DOES FIDEL EAT
MORE THAN YOUR FATHER ?

Plays by Barry Reckord

Flesh to a Tiger
You in Your Small Corner
Skyvers
Don't Gas the Blacks

DOES FIDEL EAT MORE THAN YOUR FATHER?

Conversations in Cuba

Barry Reckord

PRAEGER PUBLISHERS
New York • Washington

TO MY FATHER

BOOKS THAT MATTER

Published in the United States of America in 1971
by Praeger Publishers, Inc.
111 Fourth Avenue, New York, N.Y. 10003

© 1971 by Barry Reckord

Library of Congress Catalog Card Number: 78–146893

Printed in the United States of America

Contents

Introduction

I went to Cuba to find out how the performance there matched the rhetoric.

Few West Indians can live as emigrés in London, as I did, without feeling guilt, and mine took the form of an increasing interest in Caribbean conditions and politics: if I wasn't experiencing them I ought at least to worry about them. After coming down from Cambridge in 1953 I made the occasional trip home like a tourist; but a point comes at last — this is happening to more and more people in my situation — where the absurdity of this becomes intolerable and one decides that one must go home and at any rate try to participate in the life of one's country instead of pronouncing on it from a distance.

In Jamaica conditions now are similar to those in pre-revolutionary Cuba. People are afraid to walk in the streets after dark, and those who can afford it barricade their verandahs. According to the *Observer*, unemployment is "22 per cent nationally; perhaps 60 per cent among teen-agers", and the fear "exceeds the panic of Detroit's white suburbia" (November 23, 1969). The situation is dealt with partly by police armed with sub-machine guns, partly by double-think. Jamaica sees itself as a thriving democratic society, although according to a seminar sponsored in July 1969 by the University of the West Indies "a substantial proportion of adults have calorie intakes below 2,000 calories a day, and protein intakes below 45 grams a day — levels which are well below the allowances recommended by the United Nations."

The Daily Gleaner, the only Jamaican morning paper and the most common reading matter for Jamaicans — apart from the Bible and the *Reader's Digest* — said in a leader of March 20, 1970, that the Jamaican level of consumption is "extremely high". No distinction was made between rich and poor. "The success of most public shares issues shows that Jamaicans of all economic groups are anxious to invest their savings, whether large or small. With the increased incentive to save, it may be possible to reduce the level of consumption which is extremely high."

This is statistically accurate. On purely statistical reckoning, hunger can be averaged out; and the legion of unemployed with their bam-bellied children are living extremely high.

The Jamaican middle classes on the whole share the *Gleaner's* optimism. Used to relative poverty, they are grateful for the smallest mercies of development and concentrate on grabbing a slice of the precarious loaf. The threat remains, however, that economic growth is so marginal that it will be swallowed up by the increase in population. If Jamaicans hadn't always been able to emigrate in large numbers, there would be outright starvation for the thousands who live on money sent home from abroad. My father spent more than half his life abroad, for reasons a great deal more compelling than my own but similar to those which are still driving out most Jamaican emigrés.

What were the conditions ninety miles away in revolutionary Cuba? I kept hearing, as if they were travellers' tales, that in Cuba technology was growing rapidly, money was being abolished, people worked freely for the general good, and shared the available food. I wondered what it was like to live in a society whose first commandment was "More Conscience", not "Drink Coca-Cola". I went there to find out what Cubans thought of it.

First impressions

Militia men and women sitting leisurely guard outside public buildings; soldiers everywhere. This was one of the first things I noticed on arriving in Havana. Castro believes that Latin America must arm itself against the malevolent power of the United States, so military training has become a way of life in Cuba, and will soon be "just another subject in school". Russia has donated $1½ billion worth of arms. Most Cubans can shoot, and have a gun in the house.

How good are these soldiers? They were expert enough at Giron (the Bay of Pigs), but that was a mini-invasion. Since Cuba is still technologically backward, this might easily be a comic-opera army like the Egyptians, armed to the teeth and vulnerable; and I did overhear two Russians talking about Cuban soldiers in the bar of the Havana Libre, which used to be the Hilton; "Dancing boys?" — "More like rabble, really. A spit away from the plough." The Cuban who translated laughed.

He said, "The map has changed in America. The US for the first time tolerates a hostile military power on her doorstep. Which says something either for the Cuban army or for North American patience." I think also for the readiness of most Cubans to die if invaded. Whatever the truth, defence is certainly the first priority in Cuba. They see an inability to fight as the disease of colonialism: people helplessly accepting misery because they are cowed by local armies backed by the extraordinary power of the United States. The creation of an army marks the end of colonial psychology. It doesn't finally matter how strong the army is. The people feel strong. Cubans are prepared to fight the North Americans. Independence or death. And this is no rhetoric. Their heroes are too genuine and famous for that.

I get no impression of militarism, probably because these soldiers work like ordinary people, in factories and on farms, and because so many ordinary people are part-time soldiers. That frightening concentration on death of most armies has been destroyed. The soldiers are not a well-pressed élite with sinister smartness.

A Cuban civil servant told me that militarism hadn't developed because nothing in Cuba was properly organized as yet, but organization was coming. The same organization that was going to produce marvellous yields in agriculture might produce in the army a marvellous capacity both for defending the country and for repressing it. He was concerned about the possibility of internal repression. The only terror in the country to date he said, had been the indiscriminate round up of possible traitors, provoked by the Giron (Bay of Pigs) invasion. Most of these had been released, and there were now only a few thousand political prisoners in Cuba imprisoned for crimes not opinions. But what of the future? Suppose Fidel — fresh from agricultural triumphs — wanted to be idealistic and to intervene in Latin America, and the country, eating well for the first time, said to hell with idealism — what then? Fidel's brother Raul controlled the army. Fidel had no rivals. The *commandantes* were his men. They ate well, drove cars and would be rosy with idealism. Wouldn't the regular army threaten the people? Or suppose Fidel's agricultural policies failed, and he had to be replaced but wouldn't stand down?

I asked this man if he thought the armed population in Cuba might not serve as a defence against the abuse of internal dictatorship. "In a sense, certainly. But surely the idea of good government is that people are not obliged to face death before they can enjoy necessary change. This happens to be the position the rest of America finds itself in, and it is a miserable one. Latin Americans are shot down by reactionary pro-Yankee dictatorships any time they demand radical change. In the same way North American militants, black and white, face police terror. Cubans mustn't be obliged to face a strongman from the left."

Fidel, he said, was at least verbally aware that this was the present position, and Cuba is inching towards a democratic system where the party rules, and party members are chosen by the workers in their places of work — a one-party democracy. The two-party electoral process, he said, is geared to gradualness and is no longer practical in America which needs rapid change. For the moment, he said, Cuba has naked one-man rule, but Fidel is a genuine hero and in the opinion even of the North American press could win an election. They should ask themselves why he doesn't hold one. Is it just capriciousness, or does the third world need a new system?

This man, although not yet a party member, was a militant. The conclusion I reached, on a very rough reckoning, was that Cuba is divided into about twenty per cent militant revolutionaries, thirty per cent consumers-with-a-conscience who support the revolution, thirty per cent passive people who would support or endure any ruler, and twenty per cent blind consumers hostile to the regime — some of these for religious and political reasons as well. A handful are hostile for purely religious or political reasons.

The man I have just quoted was not a party member because, he said: "I'm too weak to leave my domestic problems at home. My wife is East European, and is bored with my going off on Sunday to do agricultural work. She says Cubans put in the hours without putting in the work or the intelligence and this is partly true, partly master-race bitchery. But basically she lacks our vision. Revolution needs imagination. My job, for example, is to distribute food. It involves the most boring office routine, twelve to fourteen hours a day, but it's necessary, and when I flag I have to remember the Latin American with his nose eaten off by disease. It is the other party members who keep me going. As I see it, one rôle of the party is to serve as the memory, the living imagination of the individual. The individual flags and forgets. The party, which is the collective individual, never flags and never forgets. That's the ideal, anyway. It works half-way. At any rate it keeps me in this country when I really long for New York, that exquisite pirate city. Next time you come we might be gone."

He wanted to go on talking, but his wife, who had joined us, started nagging about getting to the restaurant.

There is a tedious system for getting places at a restaurant. You go at about midnight and secure your place in the line. You go again next morning at six or seven to make sure your number stands a chance, then the final trip at night actually to eat the expensive food. The distribution of food in Cuba seems to me geared to forcing women out to work. There are three places to get food — home, work, restaurants — and those who work can both get a cheap meal at work and afford restaurants. Women who go out to work can leave young children in nurseries where theoretically they get everything including affection.

I walked with this man and wife to the restaurant and there was the line — black, brown and white men, labourers and white-collar types. It seemed so natural and ordinary, this miraculous Cuban equality. Nothing that anybody should need to die for. I said, "It's sheer luck that you people aren't killing each other." The wife said, "Too many lazy people here who like nothing better than to stand in line. Cuba won't be able to carry them and will have to go back to some kind of profit motive." She believed in a "punishing inequality. In Russia the wage differential is about 50–1." In Cuba it is within the public sector nominally 10–1 and broadly speaking, for all practical purposes, about 2–1. And the aim is to close the gap completely.

I went off to see M, another middle-class man who opted for the revolution. He had invited me to his house in Vedado.

The buses were overcrowded and it was a pleasant walk. Vedado used to be the kind of area you dressed up for and strolled through on a Sunday afternoon seeing how the five per cent lived: houses standing far back from the gates, distant as dreams. They were decorated with Spanish iron grille-work and looked like beautiful fortresses against the thieving poor. Now they were broken fortresses, filled with schools, working-class families, dusty shops, pre-natal clinics. Fashionable Vedado invaded by the barefoot Cuban.

I arrived at the same time as a European journalist who was here to describe Cuba for one of the continental papers and had been seeking out writers. M, looking I thought rather pleased to be sought out by a fairly important Anglo-Saxon (he obviously hadn't quite lost his Cuban inferiority complex), brought out a precious bottle of rum. Twenty dollars, he said, on the black market. Tourists get rum cheap at about $2·50 and the journalist had brought a bottle; so M, with saving pretences of every kind and many half-apologies, grabbed the man's rum. Many Cubans haven't lost their grace in twelve years but some are vultures. M was middle-aged and had been a consumer all his life. Before the revolution he worked in a civil-service sinecure five days a week, and spent Saturday wandering round book shops and record shops, never buying anything; occasionally, very occasionally, splurging on *Life* magazine. A pleasant life, disturbed by the anxious desire to make a name in the world. Tiny countries have a disproportionate number of such men. We can become known fairly easily in our own communities so we reckon this applies to the planet. We combine enormous confidence with insufficient skill and the result is a lot of day-dreaming. When I was young I wrote "If you can dream and not make dreams your master" on an exercise book in blood. It didn't help.

M's mother mortgaged her house and he went to Paris, then New York, publishing important poems in little magazines. He hit Cuba again with the revolution. Now that Castro had put Cuba on the map, an international reputation was at last feasible. He liked the Government for that. But Cuba has no book shops, no record shops to speak of. You could kid yourself with Cuban periodicals — *Cuba Socialista* or *Verde Olive* or *Tricontinental* — but they weren't *Encounter*. There was no *New York Review of Books*. Not even *Life*. You couldn't find two or three versions of the B minor mass. Often you couldn't even find one. M had an office job and he could still drift round Havana on Saturday afternoons, all day Sunday, and every day after five, but now only with a guilty conscience because he had, if not actually to work, at least to be seen to be working. He really meant to go out to the fields at least two Sundays a month, but could hardly face even one.

He could not spend a whole Sunday filling coffee bags with dirt. Even if the work lasted only half a day the whole Sunday was ruined. It was difficult when he got home to fall back into a leisurely stride. He comforted himself that Cuba needed writers, and writers needed leisure.

But there was guilt, a feeling that you were being watched and found not working. M lived in the eyes of other people. He probably didn't leave Cuba for fear of what they would think. And he wanted their approval so he'd be sent abroad on cultural missions. But his work-record had to be good and somehow he couldn't face the work, so the possibility of going abroad seemed more and more remote, yet he had to get out of Cuba from time to time. So he became fairly paralysed by the fear that he would never be sent because they secretly believed he'd skip. So here he was immured for life, his one hope to produce literature that would redeem him in the Government's eyes; his main pleasure the Anglo-Saxons who drifted his way.

We sat on the verandah in very old, very comfortable chairs and the journalist said, "I hear Cuba is making furniture in mahogany and cedar and all for export." M explained in dutiful offhand that the Cuban strategy was to hold back on consumption and buy productive goods so Cuba was rich in tractors, dams, etc, but poor in houses, cars, clothes, food and gramophone records. Tractors, of course, were badly used because of ignorance and carelessness, but these vices would gradually disappear. The journalist was silent. We had travelled together round Havana, and I knew that austerity annoyed him. It stirred up bitter memories from his childhood of promises unfulfilled, repeated disappointments. Something that was always building but never built. He really hated trusting people. "Have you ever been on a Russian collective farm?" he asked me lightly. "They don't give a fuck."

Of course he knew that they still cared in Cuba. They would get their ten million tons of sugar or something near it. But give them time. It's early days yet. He was too sophisticated actually to say it, but one could hear under his sophistication the old spiel — man by nature is individualistic; doesn't want to live in a herd, sharing goals. Man wants to be out there way ahead on his own in competition, not co-operation. He actually said, "How many examples do we need that communists are as selfish as capitalists? Look at Hungary, Czechoslovakia, and the whole communist world drifting back to capitalism. Look at China. The cultural revolution was meant to stem neo-capitalism. Mao has shipped off millions to the Gobi desert. Selfishness never ends. The jungle can at best be regulated."

M's wife came out with ice and soda. She wanted to drink and flirt and particularly not to talk about politics; not to be asked about Che for the five hundredth time. (The first time she met Che, she said, she trembled.) M wanted to bitch about other Cuban writers.

I left them to it, walked out into the Havana night hearing the screams of the dead whom Batista tortured and mutilated to destroy this revolution. Three days earlier I had met a man with no arms, no tongue, no eyes. He, obviously, couldn't say whether for him it was worth it. It suddenly occurred to me that the miracle of Cuba was that it was still in one piece. By right Cuba should be another Vietnam with its proper share of wounded and dead. Here instead was peace. Little political or criminal violence — and that in spite of all those guns. Yet the journalist hated it. Why? Because, he had argued the previous night, most dictators sooner or later end up murderous like Stalin. The one great lesson of our century was the eventual horror of totalitarianism. The Americans were brutal in Korea and Vietnam, but under protest from a lot of American people. The greatest virtue of any society was dissent. For that he would die. There was no dissent in Cuba.

I hadn't argued all night since I was at Cambridge. But in Cuba, with the problems under our nose, I argued again. The two-party system needs time, but what if you don't have the time? Do you wipe out communist agitators, and when the rot still spreads, wipe out half the nation, like in Vietnam? Do you then say: "We weren't ruthless enough with the agitators, that's the chink in our armour. We must spend all the money we need to spend blighting revolutions in the bud. The CIA must have unlimited funds."

Bourgeois society believes in democracy built up steadily over whatever time it takes, with law and order defending privilege and preventing abuses, and habit preserving us from too much envy and humiliation. Equality is not necessary. Nature clearly recognizes a pecking order. In the nineteenth century there was the rich man in his castle, the poor man at his gate. In the twentieth century there is the rich man in his Cadillac, the poor man in his Ford. That is progress. In the twenty-first century very gradually will come the turn of the black dispossessed all over the world and the end of racial prejudice. But you need patience. The world is old. Things change, not in decades but centuries. And after all, change mostly ends up the same. *Plus ça change, plus c'est la même chose.*

You can't argue with people. Sentences don't define immediately enough. In the end you simply bang the table and shout: "Food is urgent, health and housing are urgent, education is urgent, blacks want them now and fuck you Jack."

But as I walk through these Vedado streets watching the miracles I have a feeling that recurs often — what does all this really matter to me? I lapse into easy nihilism, into fun pessimism, feeling life is so apt to be brutal in so many subtle or crude ways that seriousness is ludicrous — like ants desperately tugging away at a pebble.

When I see the young men who in Jamaica would be in prison, walking here free, I say yes, yes: but nothing really happens to me. I am dead even to marvels. So all right, their bellies get fed and they are all healthy, educated, so what. I am healthy, full-bellied, full-headed and miserable. Life is tragic and nothing can change that. A revolutionary, like the man I'd talked to earlier said, needs imagination. The enemies — torture, illness, hunger, illiteracy, inferiority, gross inequality — must be always there, visible and living in his mind, nourishing indignation. The young Castro, for example, attacked the Moncada barracks and saw his friends shot

down and tortured, was sentenced to fifteen years in prison, served
two, left the country, collected arms and men, saw them shot down
and tortured, took to the mountains, continued the war against
Batista. He says it never once occurred to him to stop.

Castro has used his vices well. He has a face like a mule — a
mean-eyed mulish stubbornness and a giant-killing *machismo* which
he has harnessed to world-shaking ends. His apostle was Marti who
wrote of "the brutal North which despises us" and died fighting
for the dignity of our America.

I remember the first day I landed in England. The white man at
the immigration desk saw the name on my passport slightly fudged
and passed it to his chief who said, "It's all right. Probably done by
some bastard from the bush." I scarcely registered what was said. I
put it somewhere in the back of my mind against the day of reckoning. In the meantime I was cosmopolitan, a man of all worlds and of
none. Too hostile to whites to identify with them. Too white-
minded and well-behaved to fight them. A double alienation. Though
at the time I thought myself politically aware.

For example when I was eighteen I went to see some World War
II ex-servicemen I heard were living on the dungle in West Kingston.
The dungle is a place swarming with shanties and smelling of shit.
The ex-servicemen had been promised land and had been given a
few acres of rock-stone in the bush, so they drifted back to town and
squatted. I told them to march. We'd march in protest. I'd come the
next morning and lead (always lead) the march. But that night I
went out for the first time with a light-skinned girl. I was sexually
so green I can't imagine how the date came about. Like most West
Indians I was seriously exposed to American gospel-preachers who
at that time were concentrating on sin, and not yet mixing it with
anti-communism. I went to bed every night praying, "Make me a
clean heart oh God, and renew a right spirit within me." Which
meant no sex. I gave this girl moral advice for lack of anything to
say, and to disguise lechery. She called me Gramp (for grandpa). I
shudder at the memory. We cycled out to the Palisadoes talking
high ideals that disguised ordinary desires. What was it I said to her?

I hate to think. We sat talking and I stuck rigidly to kissing her. It never occurred to my hands to stray to her breasts. This was love, not lust. When I got home at dawn, with the moon setting, I wrote one of these poems which sixth-form colonials who read the Bible and the Romantics used to write, with 'tis and doth.

Too late doth watch the moon.
Last night beneath its cold fantastic gloom
I kissed beloved lips
And cast my soul to doom.
How loveless 'tis to pay a thousand kisses
*   with one kiss*
A thousand souls betray.
A cold fantastic moon, a golden moon
Bade Judas cast his soul away.
Tomorrow I will kiss my love beneath the moon
Lingering unto day;
Tomorrow Judas cast his soul away.

Which meant that my love, like Christ's, ought to be reserved for the thousands of poor men in the country, but lust would betray me. And I didn't turn up for the march. I woke up feeling I'd better prepare myself thoroughly, get my BA before starting on politics. God had called me to lead the world to peace and justice, but not just yet.

Some people easily take wish for deed — one day political hero, another day poet, lover, disenchanted hedonist. And all taken with great seriousness on their appointed day. What do young men like this do in Cuba? They neglect their work and die daily with Che in Latin America.

I walked down La Rampa to the Maleçon where the sea burst like fireworks over the wall. Wide wide road along the sea, running with lovers, all preternaturally the same shade. Superb, this part of town. So spotlessly clean I didn't drop my stub of cigar. Some of it dark to save electricity. Shops empty. Few cars. Walked past skyscrapers that used to be hotels for North Americans — taken over now by the natives. Students live in them. Students everywhere. Caught a black one sharply eyeing a white girl. He pretended to be eyeing her mulatto girlfriend. I know that scene well. It's a hangover from the days when white flesh was expensive. Wandered down the Maleçon towards old Havana. Dirtier and dirtier. Crowded tenements. The ghosts of pre-revolutionary Cuba. The Government has promised to refurbish these houses by 1975 ... 1985, Cuban time, which would still be better time than they're making in the North American slums.

I peer nosily into an impossibly cramped shabby room where a combo is practising and an old lady is dying on the bed. Pasted-up pictures of Jesus Christ, Che, Camillo. Books by Marx and Lenin. Next door an unrivalled virgin hostile to the regime. A lonely counter-revolutionary scrawl: "All our miracles are paid for by the Russians. The rest is Cuban." Neatly dressed children beg for chiclets. Odd, neglected child begs for money. Man I talked to said times were very much better now. Before the revolution poor children dived for coins thrown by tourists. Now the fathers all worked and the children all went to school. Full employment. Total education. As I was about to leave he asked for a cigarette, and talked about unemployment before the revolution, when there were half a million unemployed.

"I would be sitting down sick in the doorway then suddenly get up and look blindly for work in some business that I knew had nothing for me. I never moved unless I moved suddenly. I would never turn down a street on the left. Always the right. Left was bad luck. Then I'd come home and the wife would complain I was out looking for women. And then again you get used to looking but not to working, so you leave any hard job, yet you're always looking."

Everybody was working now. He swept the street. A lazy man's job, he said, and they complained he didn't do it well. He made enough to buy rations, but not really enough to go to a good restaurant. His wife could get a job but they had ten children, three of them babies. They could be put in the nursery while his wife worked, but no wife of his might leave the house. Fidel wanted women out at work, but where would that end? If they went out to work and had their own money they might as well be men. Had I seen Russian women? Monsters. These days he still had worries, but he wasn't sick with them like he used to be. The new house he lived in was a constant pleasure. So was eating regularly. But the house specially pleased him. He woke up and gazed at the ceiling. Before the revolution he woke up in mental agony wondering where to turn.

I said that before the revolution he could get a bowl of Chinese rice and shrimps for ten cents. "Yes, but with eight children . . . " One of them would always need new shoes. Once he stole the shoes. They didn't fit. He cut them up in a rage and from a secret calculation that the police wouldn't find them. Nowadays his wife put a picture of Fidel over the stove, but she really thought the revolution was a miracle from the Virgin. He himself resented the years of his life religion had wasted — he'd like to drive a pile up a priest's bum. His eldest son was nearly a doctor and did I know Cuba had a doctor for every thousand people, which was better than the US.

I said to this street-sweeper, "Why do people want to leave Cuba?"

"*Gusanos* [worms]. They are *gusanos*. *Gusanos*."

"How many want to leave?"

He had no idea and he didn't like the turn of the questioning. He felt it might be hostile to the revolution and left.

I kept thinking he was born articulate, this man. Talk to poor people about poverty and they usually have nothing to say. You're moved by the dumb acceptance. They accept any system, take what they get, and live.

I reckon about one out of every three of the people I met in Cuba was so politically backward that they scarcely knew or cared what the Government was doing. Their energies are consumed in private quarrels, family feuds. They have no time for public interests. These are not important. Witchcraft is important. I asked a woman bitten by a dog if she got anti-tetanus injections and tablets. She said yes, but what really helped was putting her hand on the altar

and pulling it off hot, hot. So many mediaeval people still live in
Cuba. They accept Fidel as they accepted Batista — absentmindedly.
I asked this woman about her new house. "I was a victim of flood
and mud and they move me into this house. They call a meetin'
and say de house is yours and how to keep de house. They show
you round, you know. The toilet is inside and that is unsanitary,
but I can put up with that. They say the house is mine but still I
never knew for certain sure how long I would be there. It wasn't my
house you understand. So at first all day I just sit in the house and
consider about what the future would be. I might get move out
again because people will whisper things to the Government
against me. [She whispers.] You see is only me and husband and
three children, and plenty big families need house. So how long
will I be here for? I know everybody in these new houses feel nice
and bright, jumpin' round, servin' out their little coffee to friends
and findin' out everybody business. I keep my coffee. Any day I
might be out in the street because those brutes gang up on me, and
talk to the Government. And of course plenty outside don't get
house and want house. And my husband not even here frequently
so I just keep my mouth to meself and go to my work every day.
[She sews.] All my life everything have something. When I have de
frock I don't have de booze. When I have de booze, I don't have de
frock. So all my life I expect nutten different. But you think with
Nixon in now Castro will fall? I lookin' for him to fall and losin' me
house. If dey launch real invasion, what you think? If dey send
Americans, not just Cubans. Or if dey back up de Cubans wid
plenty plenty Americans — what you think? I could go back to the
slum any time because that would be mine. I could put it up meself,
me one, because my husband is a worthless black man. [She is
white.] And I keep it nice. I never let my baby piss on de bed. In a
pail all de time. And see me dress up at night you couldn't know
where I crawl out. But me last baby died. My husband say we get
the house because the baby dead and every cloud have it line."

This woman in her fearful way supported Fidel, but a good
twenty per cent of the people here don't give a damn about schools,

hospitals or technology, or trust the promises of future plenty, so they want to leave and eat now in Miami. There is a cold war in Cuba between a strong idealistic government and an army of chronic consumers who spend their days in lines and their nights in petty black marketeering and barter deals, swapping rum for shoes, cigars for soap, and jokes about the Government. "Fidel consulted his dead mother through a medium. 'My mother, are the people with me this year?' — 'Yes my son, this year with you, next year with me.' " One lady in a line told me that God was punishing Cuba for something it had done in the past, and Fidel was God's minister. These are the twenty per cent who actively or passively want to leave.

An upper-class girl — a pretty girl but careless of her looks, and tense — five minutes after she met me proposed, only half in fun, that we have a platonic wedding so she could leave the country. She was sick of endless lines where you rub with morons. No clothes. Little food. Was she hungry now? — "Yes." What had she eaten that day? — "An egg, a lot of bread and cassava, a little fish, coffee." — Wasn't this a lot of food by Latin American standards, and wasn't it incredible that everybody should be getting at least this? She said she had less than she was used to; she had sacrificed ten years of her life, that was enough.

It wasn't only food and clothes this girl cared about. She felt the new Cubans hated her class. She hadn't left Cuba with the rest of her family because she had been a revolutionary, had given up her house out of revolutionary zeal and married a peasant. He wouldn't live with her when she turned out not to be a virgin. She lived in a tenement, sharing with hostile oafs who had a bad habit of appearing from nowhere, frightening hell out of her. It got to the stage where she jumped even when they weren't there. Her husband came to lay her the odd night, leaving next morning without saying very much. She got pregnant, and the night she started labour went out into the streets to get a cab. The streets were empty and blocked off for some political celebration. The police took her to hospital. "Didn't you have any friends?" — "Yes, office-friends, but none of them showed the slightest concern." And then she said: "People are cruel in any system. Systems make no difference." Occasionally she suffered from a consumer-goods trauma — insistent feelings that her old dress was dirty, wanting to tear it off, fling her old shoes into the sea to get them new and clean and release her feet. She would tear home to get back to American broadcasts in English.

An extraordinary girl. She had visited China and had wanted to go and fight against imperialism in the Congo. And here she was now. I reminded her of the children burning up in Vietnam. She said wearily, "Yes, I know all about them." I said that starvation means nausea and belly-ache and a life dominated by illness and premature death. That Cuba was the best hope in America for changing this. She said she'd crawl on hands and knees to get out of Cuba.

Even some poor people who are much better off now than they were before the revolution find the new system traumatic. They had spent their lives buying at the Chinaman shop on the corner whenever they had the money, which wasn't often. Now they had to line up and this they weren't used to. Hunger seems preferable to ration-book food. As a result many poor people are hostile to the revolution. Their chronic animal habits have been broken. They feel fractured, move about like displaced people. They feel holed-up in an unfamiliar prison and occasionally become desperate — like the truckload of people who recently crashed into the American base at Guantanamo for refuge.

It is hard to get out of Cuba in any other way. The US used to send a plane daily to take out people who wanted to leave, and the Cuban Government allowed this, but then the US cut down the flights to one a week. This means a long waiting list and it takes two or three years to get out this way. There are Cubana Airline flights to Mexico twice a week, and for these you wait only nine months, but you have to know somebody abroad, who has to send you a ticket. The same goes for the weekly flight to Madrid. And the moment you announce you want to leave, you lose your job and ration-book and must work in the fields on the basis that anybody who wants to leave must grow the food they and their children eat.

This goes on till you leave. When you go you have to abandon your property because even if the Government were to buy it, there would be no point taking out money which instantly became useless. Jewellery one ought to be allowed to take, but one isn't. Boys between sixteen and twenty-six can't leave the country. They are of military age and the Government doesn't want to swell the ranks of Cubans who may be recruited in Miami for invading Cuba. Besides, ten years gives the Government a chance to change the boy's thinking. But apart from all these reasons, the real difficulty about leaving Cuba, the issue of over-riding importance, is that families are always divided about leaving. The wife wanting to leave has to reckon with husband, daughter or son who supports the new Cuba. This rending of families is distressing. In this revolution the middle-classes haven't been killed off, only separated.

I talked to a woman whose husband had left for Miami. "Happiness?" she said. "Happiness is for children. Adults have other concerns." She was one of the twenty per cent who actively work for the revolution. She was a technician in a factory, was out to see production go up and nothing could make her leave Cuba. When I asked her about the food shortages she said, "How can I change my ideas for pork?" In private this girl was a bitch: selfish, devious, slightly colour-prejudiced. I got the impression her interest in watching production figures in the factory go up and up was miserly. She was no new man. And in a sense there are few new men in Cuba. Not much private virtue. Only a spectacular collective virtue.

The individual who is unjust works in a society that shares its food fairly evenly, doesn't discriminate against blacks, gives priority to hospitals and schools over Cadillacs and mansions, wipes out unemployment with the money it borrows. The society is moral, even if the individual is not. Men are more just, more humane in a collective sense.

The only individual virtue really demanded is work. Work, work,

work. The word dominates the Cuban front page. Thousands of men going out every day to the bush, to chop it down or plough it up. You see them at the airport, flying off to the cane-fields, machete neatly clasped in briefcase, like going to the office, only it's to the brute business of levelling cane, a torturing ritual got through God knows how, in the hope that you can stick it till the day's end. It breaks the will, cutting cane. I comfort myself it's a business for masochists. Ordinary men come to fear it. Some of them spend ten months in the office quietly dreading a possible two months in the field, carefully calculating how it could be turned into one.

I asked a friend of mine whether he cut cane. He said shortly, "Enough." Why does he go? Because there is moral pressure on him to go. But it is *moral* pressure. If he has no morality he needn't go. He can stay in the office and still draw his salary. There is a legal necessity to go to the fields only one day a week. You get the day off from the office, and if you don't go you aren't paid. But most people go not only once a week, but one or two Sundays a month and a month or two each year. The militant twenty per cent set the work pace in Cuba and most of the country follows. In a factory of two hundred people, twenty or so party militants decide that it is necessary to work four hours extra a day for several weeks to get the work done, so a general meeting is called and hey presto the vote is unanimous. The hostile twenty per cent neither attend nor do the extra work. They get cold-shouldered, called *gusano*, a lift attendant might force them to walk up the stairs. Food gets roughly shovelled on to their plate in the canteen.

In hierarchical societies like the US, and Russia, where there is a belief in material incentives and managers earn far more than most workers, the Cuban reliance on voluntary labour is inconceivable. You can't ask people to work long hours for nothing when some of them will benefit less than others. In a Cuban factory there is basic equality. Where somebody is getting less it's often the manager. Profits from the work done don't go on summer resorts for party functionaries. Not yet, anyhow. There is a thin red line of privilege in Cuba but it is very thin, goes with a very exacting job, and is not yet creating a new class. So Cuban militants feel free to demand as much work as is necessary.

Perhaps the most definable thing about the new man in Cuba is that he is vitally concerned with agriculture. His ruling passion is increased production, so that America may eat. His new morality is work. Sexual morality is secondary. Party members are expected to stick to one woman, be it girlfriend or wife, because love-affairs take time. If you're always philandering the party begins to wonder where your true interests lie — work or women? It can scarcely be both if you work sixteen hours a day and have a wife and children. If you drink or gamble till early morning the same question arises. You meet dozens of people not yet able to join the party because they are still private men whose primary concerns are emotional — changing wives, running a heart-ache, unable to leave women who don't want them to go out to the fields on a Sunday. In the party private affections are not paramount. Wife and husband are away from home working long hours; children are often brought up at their most impressionable age in a public nursery. It was revealing to watch women who longed for their husbands and children, and who were also devoted party people. The solution invariably was for everybody to get less sleep. Four or five hours instead of eight or nine. You come home at nine and stay up till one with the children.

Astonishing, this armed conscience in Cuba! Three million party members or aspiring party members, most of them young, take it for granted that poverty, illiteracy and disease must go, and are ready to work (and die if necessary) in the fight against them. The end of verandah socialism. They work long hours a day believing that work is the only way to honour their dead heroes. No one who doesn't work freely has any right to pay tribute to Che. To raise the question of overtime is sacrilege, like buying and selling in a temple. When you go into a factory of two hundred people and find twenty or thirty of them who work ten hours in the factory, then another three hours building a school across the street, then study for two or three hours — and who get so used to working at this pitch that they are always busy fifteen hours a day, for no reward

except the honour of being party members or vanguard workers —
then you are meeting the new man in Cuba. An increasingly
efficient person, dead set to wipe out tragic abuses. Tell these
people that Fidel's planning is often seriously mistaken and they
say, "Yes, Cubans are still ignorant and inefficient after centuries of
colonialism, and it might take a generation to create abundance."

Till then the dominant ideal in Cuba is physical work; which
makes it a boring place for prosperous Westerners whose ideal is the
white-collar job and a four-day week. There are problems on factory
and farm that need a grappling intelligence, but on the whole
machine-minding and hacking away at sugar-cane are dull, and the
only thing that makes it possible for intelligent young people to do
them is habit and the principles involved: work-sharing, avoiding a
labouring class, building the first free territory in Latin America
and finally burying capitalism.

Liberty

"Sr Castro's attitude confirms the alternatives of the revolutionary process in Latin America. Either his system, based on the capricious dictatorship of one man, without elections and without a parliament, with only one party, an official press, no liberty, thousands of firing-squad executions and with satellite-type political and economic dependence abroad; or the revolution with freedom elected by Chile in 1964, with free elections and an open parliament where all currents of opinion are represented, with a free press and radio, with freedom within unions, and with an active political opposition."

So Sr Frei, former premier of Chile. To find out what Cubans thought I decided to case a few blocks. Knock on any door, walk in and talk. My first stop was a meeting of a CDR (Committee for the Defence of the Revolution). The majority of the people on any block are members of the CDR. These committees were once vigilance units against counter-revolutionaries, the eyes and ears of the block, then gradually started serving other functions. Usually plans for concrete action are worked out at meetings: who will check on a delinquent child or help in an understaffed shop. But while plans are being made complaints get aired, and now a young man was saying that stocks of matches arriving in the shops were damp. Failure to deliver replacements on time led to panic and hoarding, so existing stocks ran out. There was also a shortage of paraffin (kerosene) so people had to leave food lying about, with no fuel to cook it. Also the milk came at eight one morning, eleven the next, and then at four the following afternoon

The young man got the standard answer to all complaints —
comrades had to be out in agriculture so things got messed up: after
all, the ten million tons were vital — this tremendous sugar-cane
harvest to which Cuba was pledged for 1970. The meeting seemed
to go along with this explanation from the chairman, some willingly,
some blankly, some thinking their own thoughts. The chairman said
people knew they were better off than ever before, look at all the
things that were free: homes, hospitals, schools and school meals,
telephones, transport. A worker from the back said people spoke
their minds in Cuba and he was speaking his mind: anybody who
didn't like the shortages could swim to Key-West. The people
laughed.

He said: "Havana people are crazy. They want everything for
Havana. They complain about shortage of running water and electric
light bulbs when our people in the country still go to the well, and
don't know what electricity is!"

There was vigorous nodding, and a little spontaneous clapping.
The worker stood up with the encouragement and quoted Fidel:
"More day-to-day heroism, comrades." Applause. A fat woman,
bloated with a starchy diet and fed up with the hours of queuing,
fetched a deep sigh and looked away. The worker was incredulous
that there could be any complaining.

"Before the revolution there were how many hospitals in rural
Cuba? One. With how many beds? A dozen. Now there are fifty,
comrades. Now there are fifty! We have a developed medicine. The
greatest in the world. And much less crime. Why are we worrying
about matches and paraffin?" He said he was against too much
liberalism, too much patience with complainers and *gusanos*. He
wanted to whip them all the way to Miami. The people applauded
and the young teacher, no *gusano* but cornered by the herd, lashed
out.

"People do *not* speak their minds. We are not allowed to protest
against the Russian invasion of Czechoslovakia. Everybody is hush-
mouthed about Fidel's speech on it. Fidel does all our thinking.
How the hell can you call that speaking out?"

Passionate uproar. The chairman said, "Be polite comrades." A woman said: "Elections are the will of Yankee people, not our will."

"Who said anything about elections?" said the young teacher. The woman shouted: "You know what Fidel says; if he change and get old and miserable like Mao and we have to shoot him, then every man has a gun in his house." A woman near me, supporting the teacher, seemed exasperated at ordinary people putting their mouth into things. The worker from the back said to great applause that the purest democracy in the world was here in Cuba. The CDRs were the assemblies of the people.

"In *this* CDR," said the teacher, "everything gets swept under the carpet for as long as possible." The worker said it was right for things to be swept under for as long as possible since Cuba faced many difficulties. But Fidel knew what things were bad, and look — weren't the lines getting shorter? Nobody seemed to think they were, but they cheered him. The chairman said there was free criticism in Cuba. Even *gusanos* could say what they liked in the CDR though they preferred to complain in the bus, the free bus. Demonstrations weren't allowed in Cuba because there was urgent need of unity; the Government had earned the right to demand unity because it served the common interest whether or not it made mistakes. Every system, of course, had its dangers. Electoral politics in the US meant the sort of painfully slow change that took a heavy toll in poverty, disease, crime and the wasted lives of jail and drugs. Then he soothed the teacher, saying everybody was aware of the shortages, and of course steps were being taken. He closed by promising that the queues would soon be getting shorter, everybody seemed pleased, and the meeting passed on to other business.

I had come to Cuba thinking that there was the dictatorship of one party and of one man within that party. But here were revolutionary Cubans saying that these CDR assemblies were "the purest democracy in the world"; that they approved of Fidel, and he was answerable to them because they were armed. "The CDRs," the chairman told me after the meeting, "are an armed, politically aware and growing majority, and they can be counted."

Cuban thinking about the CDRs appears to be that they answer the democratic formula of consent, and that Cuba now has a constitutional set-up in which a countable majority approves of its leader and leaves him to choose a government; and that is a far cry from Sr Frei's "capricious dictatorship of one man without elections and without a parliament". But if the CDRs answer the question of consent, there is still unanswered the equally vital question of peaceful succession.

Fidel's own version of the CDR as an example of new, spontaneous, grass-roots democracy also reveals his awareness of an unfinished process: "Some may raise the question: do you have a genuine socialist constitution? And we would answer no, we don't have any socialist constitution. What then is the state constitution? It is the old bourgeois constitution to which the revolution has made numerous amendments. That is, we have a piece of socialist legislation on the base of a bourgeois constitution.

"Our revolution did not wish, for example, to start off by creating in the abstract an impressive so-called socialist constitution. And how glad we are! How happy we are!

"In the light of present experience, and looking back over the immense darkness of our past ignorance, we see with absolute clarity how many unrealistic ideas and abstractions a thousand leagues from reality such a constitution would have involved. And when our country is in its tenth, eleventh or twelfth year of revolution, in 1969 or 1970, when we decide to draw up a constitution imbued with the aspirations of this revolutionary process, it will doubtless not be a flawless creation; but it will be infinitely superior to what we could have drafted in the first few months of 1959.

"In what classic of revolutionary ideas was such an institution as the CDR mentioned? In what program, in what manifesto, in what declaration, was such an institution as this ever mentioned? It is not found in books. In a constitution drafted in 1959 we could not have been able to say one word of what has now become one of the most fruitful creations of our revolution. The Defence Committee would not even have appeared.

"If suddenly there were no Defence Committees, if suddenly they did not exist, how many fundamental tasks that this organization carries out today would be left undone in all fields, in all senses.

"The Defence Committees now take part in the job of preventing diseases that, caught in time, can be checked or ameliorated, their terrible consequences averted. The struggle for the people's health thus becomes perfected, more effective and more profound from one year to the next. And the rôle of this institution has been decisive in these victories. Its rôle in education is decisive, and the part it plays in production is increasingly outstanding.

"But recently the rôle of the Committees for the Defence of the Revolution is moving towards new forms of social institutions, towards new liaison mechanisms between the masses and the governing institutions, towards the development of genuinely new and efficient forms of democracy. And in the long run we will conclude by perfecting these mechanisms. We will conclude, in the first place, by discovering the most suitable social mechanisms for each thing. But if we know how to put our experiences of reality to good use, we will be able to find them in all spheres, in all parts."

The Cuban thesis is that problems like peaceful succession must be solved gradually and that in the meantime democracy is as democracy does: the Government is engaged in popular projects carried out by the masses. If the CDRs grow and work, then this is a sign of a healthy democracy: a fair claim so far as it goes. Perhaps the Cuban people didn't *choose* Castro, but clearly the majority approves of him. If these same assemblies ever get restless and want to throw out the Government, hopefully some simple device will be worked out, such as taking a vote in the CDRs. And the army? Fidel on several occasions has talked about an armed people trained to defend their liberty; but one isn't sure that in fact they wouldn't be disarmed by the regular army before they could possibly agree on any action.

I discussed this with a medical student living in a small room with his French girlfriend: a stocky, earnest young man with a passion for theory. Did he think the army was becoming something of a vested interest and might be used to terrorize the Cuban people? Well, he said, the Pentagon was a vested interest. Things wouldn't be any worse than the terror against the Black Panthers in the States.

I said the Panthers were a tiny minority.

"Are you a Panther?"

"No, I'm not even an American."

"If you were North American, would you be a Panther?"

"No."

"Why not?"

"Too old, too nervous."

He suddenly seemed busy, perhaps because, being black himself, he was sure he would have been a Panther, and perhaps also because I had barged in. He saw me out. I stood in the street getting my bearings and a man passed, muttering "Why can't I get a drink; I want a fucking drink." A moment later the medical student ran down the stairs, frantically in search of someone who turned out to be me. He was greatly relieved when he saw me. He felt guilty about being so abrupt and about not making the right point.

Once we had got going he began to revel in discussion, and we talked on and off for the next few days. Unlike most Cubans who simply laugh at any concern about liberty in Cuba, he staked out the theoretical position of what he called a one-man democracy. He said one-man democracy must be distinguished from one-man rule. In one-man rule a bad ruler, who might even be popular, held a country by force and/or ignorance — like Papa Doc Duvalier in Haiti, or Trujillo in the Dominican Republic. In such a system legislation made little difference to the condition of the people. But in one-man democracy a popular leader legislated in the common interest. Legislation was really the test of democracy, not the number of rulers or chambers. As for terror, he said, it wasn't dictatorship that made countries prone to terror, but crisis. If there was deep crisis in the US, and threat of invasion, all her famous constitutional safeguards would vanish; and conversely constitutional safeguards were no guarantee against crisis. As a rule any democracy that suffers military defeat and economic disaster tears up its constitution. Might not a genuine Soviet threat against the US in the fifties have brought the fascist Joe McCarthy to power? Even with scarcely any threat, there were serious tremors for three or four years. Critics of the Cuban dictatorship should also look at the crisis the country faces — blockaded by a powerful neighbour.

If there was no crisis in Cuba, he said, if she was secure and prosperous and Fidel then wanted to invade Venezuela against the wishes of the Cuban people, then he would face the same sort of problems as some new Yankee McArthur who wanted to continue the Vietnam war on his own against people's wishes with the support of the army. The Yankee people might even be more helpless than the Cuban people who are trained in arms almost to a man.

The most genuine democracy was not democratic constitutions, but democratic institutions — schools that teach everybody, hospitals that serve all equally, progress towards reasonably equal work and living conditions for everybody, and above all a politically aware people trained in arms. But can these things, he asked, be achieved where there are vested bourgeois interests? Measure democracy not by the number of rulers but by the number of these vested interests: where there are strong vested interests there isn't likely to be democracy. In any capitalist country high profits were more urgent than fair distribution and there was never enough emphasis on the people's education and health. The result was New York City, which the Yankees were only proud of because, ironically, capitalism generated the pessimism which was its best defence.

The two-party system, he said, is unsatisfactory in fundamental ways. It has no answer to the question of large minorities, since its only concern is majority rule. These minorities are exploited or wished away or both, and there is a drift to racism. This was the position in the US and Europe. In Cuba, where twenty-five per cent of the population is black, there was no racial problem for many reasons, one of which was that there were no demagogic elections appealing to people's worst instincts and stirring up hatred.

Moreover, one man one vote doesn't even guarantee the will of a majority. It is based on the mythical freedom of the individual and his enlightened self-interest. It disguises the loaded influence of press and television owned by a wealthy minority and playing on a largely ignorant population. In the US and Europe, what proportion of the working class goes to a university? The masses probably don't even regard a university education as important because their tastes are created by commercial interests. The position is worse in colonies. Pre-revolutionary Cuba, with its famous constitutional guarantees, was an undemocratic country with an exploited majority. Neither was there much gradual peaceful progress. There was less primary education in the fifties than in the twenties.

Also, he said, bourgeois elections appeal to purely national interest. US commerce has benefited from four major wars in this century. The Yankee people as a whole suffer from these wars because of higher taxes, but big business benefits, exploiting the chauvinism that comes naturally to most people. The appeal to conscience is an up-hill job, beyond the capacity and against the interests of a commercial society.

It was obvious, he said, that bourgeois constitutional ideas might have to be re-thought in the third world — for example the function of the press. In a country like the United States of America, full of conflicting, selfish and powerful interests, a free press is necessary to discover abuses and make them public. In Cuba, where there is a broad common interest and the need for rapid change, criticism must come from within a united party, and there seems no good reason why any of it should be published. The need for regular elections also needed re-thinking. While a ruler was efficient and popular, surely the longer he ruled, the better? It was only in places where office was a matter of spoils that the spoils had to be rotated. Serious revolutions engaged in fundamental and long-term reconstruction, which is prone to error, need patience and unity and internal criticism, not elections every four years. In a revolution leaders often hang on to power because any threat to the leader is a threat to the whole system. Once the system becomes relatively stable then, theoretically, they can step down gracefully, witness Malenkov and Khrushchev.

As for the separation of powers, in the US the Courts might be separate and free but the laws were bourgeois laws that took savage inequality and capitalism absolutely for granted.

The essence of bourgeois democracy, he said, is the belief that government exists to protect business, so nobody in the US thinks it strange that businessmen finance presidential campaigns. Liberty boils down to discovering or creating people's needs, and fulfilling them, so better some industrious capitalist making a profit by providing a service in a free market, than some communist bureau-crat armed with a gun and a slogan, and as privileged as any capitalist. It was right to fear bureaucracy. The genius of Castro, he claimed, is that he has destroyed a parasitic bureaucracy. So Cuba now combines high production (in agriculture) with fair dis-tribution and enjoys a whole new range of freedoms — e.g. rationality and a living conscience.

Why, he asked, was terror thought to be endemic in communism? Linking communism with Stalinist terror was like linking capitalism with the child-hanging of the industrial revolution. There was no inherent connexion. To come to Cuba looking for terror was like walking round New York looking for a little gallows. Communism, like capitalism, developed from primitive and savage beginnings. Stalin's need to industrialize and collectivize rapidly raised vast unfamiliar problems, and there was the same threat of attack that faces Cuba. But Cuban, like Chinese, communists, logically bene-fited from Russian experience and progress. The most important single factor in the Cuban revolution was finding a steady and steadily increasing market in Russia for Cuban sugar. The lack of such markets for Latin American products resulted in more starva-tion, illness and death for Latin America than ever took place under Stalin. The Yankees wage economic terror in Latin America. Of course the idea that Cuba had swapped Yankee for Russian dominance was a common one, but as Fidel says, the Russians don't own an acre of Cuba. The Yankees used to own Cuba. The Russians provide suitable markets and substantial low-interest loans. Not the Yankees. If Russian help was meant to increase Russian influence in Latin America, then so much the better.

Here I should perhaps point out that the popular view that the Russian sugar deal with Cuba is charity is probably false. According to Réné Dumont, the French agronomist, "some people work out the average cost of [sugar-beet] production in the Soviet Union at higher than sixteen cents a pound. If this is true the cost in the USSR would be over three times the Cuban cost and would far exceed both world market prices and prices paid to Cuba." (Che went even further, wondering on what basis one assesses the price of goods produced with a machete in the hot sun as against goods produced in automated factories.) And in spite of her imports of Cuban sugar, the USSR increased production of beet-sugar between 1960 and 1965 by more than thirteen per cent per annum (Statistical Abstract of the United States, 1967, page 877, quoted by Huberman and Sweezy in *Socialism in Cuba*). In this respect Cuba pays her way, and the chief reason for the determination of Cubans to produce ten million tons of sugar in 1970 was that it would help the balance of payments and strengthen the country's independence.

My friend the medical student wondered where the North American reputation as champions of liberty came from. They wiped out Indians, seized Texas by butchering Mexicans, and enslaved black men. Even a brutal terror like Stalin's, he said, lasted only five or six years (*sic*). Compare the long terror in the South and the black ghettoes. And why were even the whites so grateful to capitalism? It brutalizes them. They go off and fight impossibly brutal wars because they hope to come out alive. They accept semi-literacy because it doesn't stop them eating. They accept wage slavery because they have a car to come and go in. It often doesn't even occur to them that there's a problem. As a result the place to look for terror is the United States. Stalin carted away millions because millions raised hell. Well, let black men raise hell in the States and they'll be carted away. Let blacks behave like the kulacks and they'll be sunk.

We ended up talking about personal liberty. He said he couldn't live in a country where he had to toe the line. In Cuba it wasn't necessary to be a member of the Young Communists to be allowed to study medicine. In fact he was a Catholic. Yes, he went to Mass. He spent a lot of time trying to reconcile his politics with his religion. He was mystified about the US attitude to liberty. Was there some elusive thing which they understood about liberty and he didn't?

I said they were worried, for example, about how voluntary was the voluntary work in Cuba. Youngsters of fifteen were drafted into the army, paid eight pesos a month pocket-money, and made to cut cane.

He said all young Cubans in or out of the army cut cane or did agricultural work as part of their education. They all learnt to cut cane like they learnt to fire a gun or do mathematics. In the army they worked and studied. When he was in the army they cut cane as voluntarily as they did sums or read literature. It was part of the time-table and some were keen, some lazy. The daughters of peasants particularly hated farm-work and were always finding the shade. Cuba was no longer a bourgeois country where the point of education was to avoid physical work, but the old mentality died hard.

He himself took voluntary work absolutely for granted since he'd done it all through school and university. It was part of life.

What he hated about cutting cane was the dormitory living, with its inane conversation and endless practical jokes that seemed occasionally to have an edge of class-hatred. But these things made bitterly clear to him the intolerable divisions still existing in Cuban society between the educated and the semi-literate, and *that*, he said, must end, "even if I have to cut cane forever".

He said he found himself disliking a few busy people busily climbing into the party, who had no talent; but he had to remember that at least they did hard physical work, harder than his. And what did it matter if they talked a lot of nonsense? Talk wasn't important in Cuba. In the cane-field any bureaucrat who gives orders that lead to confusion is exposed. You need real talent. Fidel, he said, is working the Cuban bureaucrats to death. Destroying them by work.

Among the chief internal threats to Cuban liberty are these bureaucrats who, given their head, would make bad plans, impoverish the country, and use force to curb discontent.

There was a time when people in the US feared that they might be outproduced in consumer goods by a planned, regimented and efficient Soviet production machine, but that was before they knew about the inefficiency of bureaucracy. Bureaucrats have neither capitalist incentives nor socialist conscience. Castro defines them as chronic white-collar types who are averse to manual work, never leave their offices, and are too remote from problems generally to make sound plans. Bureaucracy, he has said, is almost as dangerous an enemy as imperialism. His cure is to have worker-intellectuals, who know the job from the ground up, and the Cuban revolution has taken massively to working and studying. Fidel himself has become knowledgeable in agriculture and animal genetics. His plan is eventually to have everybody working four hours and studying four hours, in universities built round farms and factories.

"The day must arrive when our entire working population must be composed of highly-trained personnel. But when the entire working mass is highly-trained, the division between manual workers and intellectual workers will have disappeared. One day society will no longer be composed of ignorant people on the one hand doing the hardest physical labour, and production intellectuals on the other in white collar and tie. In the future everyone will be in shirt-sleeves, or if they like in collar and tie at a machine. Within twenty or thirty years the technologically prepared personnel in this country will be counted by the hundreds of thousands. It is enough to point out that by the year 1970 the number of students in secondary schools, senior high schools, technological schools and Universities will be half a million. And this means that within a few years more, we will be able to say that in this country every citizen is technologically trained on at least a twelfth grade level.

"There are some technocrats of education who, never having conceived this possibility, still live the old concepts and ask, 'and who is going to perform the tasks of production?' The technicians, with their hands! In accordance with this the need to handle tractors and other equipment has been established among the students of the Agricultural Technological Institutes.

"Who would have thought, seven years ago, of speaking of half a million secondary students? None. But it so happens that reality exceeds the most optimistic estimates. When we referred to this some people exclaimed: 'What? And who is going to produce our material goods?' But is society forever going to be divided between monopolists of knowledge and monopolists of ignorance, so that the monopolists of knowledge live in collar and tie in air-conditioned offices, and the monopolists of ignorance — the immense majority of the population — have to perform the most brutalizing work?" (*Granma*, February 26, 1967.)

Socialism has for a long time faced the problem that the division of labour between workers and planners tends to end up in a division of power and privilege. Marx talked about workers' representatives being "working-bodies not talking-shops" and Lenin quoted him, but the difficulty is that as long as workers leave intellectuals to do their thinking and planning they'll remain an exploited class, and it will be merely sentimental to equate workers by hand and brain, even if they get the same wages. It's no use, either, calling on intellectuals to dirty their hands from time to time, because on the whole they'll dirty them less and less. The need is not for planners mixing in occasionally with the workers to learn the ropes or show willing, but for worker-intellectuals who can do their own planning.

At present Cuban workers are very much at the mercy of planners who dirty their hands cutting cane two weeks a year and on the occasional Sunday; also very much at the mercy of Fidel's benevolence. Fidel appears to be aware of the situation, and is belting ahead with educational plans aimed at ending the difference between "monopolists of knowledge" and "monopolists of ignorance". In the Soviet Union students *do* practical work. In Cuba workers and students will increasingly *be* the same people.

In the meantime, till this day arrives, Cuban leaders are supposed not to be petit-bourgeois collar and tie brethren, but revolutionaries who "go into the factories, into production units, rooting out everything that hinders progress, solving problems" (Fidel).

Anybody can foresee the results of this breezy inspirational work-style on the tidy bureaucratic mind. Fidel sweeps in, roots out something, plans get changed every month, production sometimes falls, people are irritated and pride is hurt. Among Cuban planners today, swallowing pride is the cardinal revolutionary virtue, and not an easy one in a people given to *machismo*. A few resign, leave the country, work with cool spite for the CIA, commit suicide. (When one Minister of Labour killed himself his best friend said to a friend of mine, "How could he do that to Fidel?")

In a speech congratulating steel-workers who had built eight hundred harrows in twenty-three days Castro showed the happier results of this work-style.

"The accomplishments which we are honouring today certainly could not pass unnoticed . . . Possibly no one would have believed that so much equipment could be produced in so short a time. And why was such an effort necessary? . . . The use of heavy machinery to clear the land is often useless if harrows are not put to work immediately afterwards. Without the work of the harrows, the efforts we have made in the work of bulldozing would have remained incomplete throughout the countryside.

"This situation has become more and more serious. On January 25, while we were visiting the provinces of Las Villas and Camaguey, we were able to observe the critical need for this type of equipment. Therefore, we presented the problem. The Ministry of Industry was informed that there was an imperative and urgent need for such equipment and that production of harrows should begin that very day. This is the type of thing we must always be ready to do and we must always be prepared to find a solution to such problems. In such a vast and dynamic agricultural development program, such bottlenecks may arise at any time. And when such problems come up they must be solved, just as this problem was solved, on the spot.

"The work began January 25, not just on heavy 17,000-pound harrows but also on 10,000-pound harrows. And in record time, just twenty-three days, the eight hundred harrows needed were produced . . .

"Two things made this extraordinary project possible: the revolutionary spirit of our steel-workers and the style and method of work followed by the leadership in the Ministry of Industries.

"This is a good example of what can be done when revolutionary methods of leadership are employed, of what can be accomplished when bureaucratic red tape is avoided. We know that during these twenty-three days, the Comrade Minister of Industries, leaders of this branch of production, and all who in one way or another could help, have been in close contact with or present in the centres of production involved. I feel sure that not only has an important goal been reached, but that this experience has also contributed to creating and strengthening in the comrades at the Ministry a revolutionary work-style, a work-style that all the ministries should employ. I feel sure they have had a fine opportunity to see all that can be accomplished with the workers, how a contagious enthusiasm can be created, and how an *esprit de corps* capable of overcoming any obstacle can be created. We who have been waging a long fight against bureaucracy and the bureaucratic spirit must be grateful for what this effort and the fulfilment of this goal has meant. I am going to repeat here something I said recently at a meeting with party comrades and others who hold posts of responsibility in agriculture in the province of Santa Clara. I said that we, in respect to our deserving the name of revolutionary, failed in one respect, early in the revolution: and that failure consisted in not doing away with the ministries . . . It is not that the economy can exist without guidance;

rather, guidance cannot exist within the old concept of ministries that we inherited.

"And under the old concept, what is a ministry first of all? In the first place, it is a large building, eight, ten, twelve, fourteen, or fifteen stories high; and in the second place it's full of people. And in the third place, it is the diagrammatic concept of life, blind faith in the virtues of paper work, of the organizational diagram and the office. But suffice it to say that from an office we would not have learned on January 25 of the problem that existed with the harrows.

"What aroused the enthusiasm of the workers in the various enterprises that participated in this plan? . . . Was it an organizational diagram? It wasn't the paper-work; it was the spirit, the antithesis of paper-work, offices and even organizational diagrams . . . It is not hard to make organograms. A line here, three there, squares and more squares. It develops in someone's mind, as an idea, a sheer abstraction. Someone feels that life must adjust to this diagram. And instead of trying to adjust the forms of organization to life, he tries to adjust life to those abstract forms of organization. And that's how everything gets tangled up. When we speak of eliminating the ministries, we are referring to elimination of this concept.

"I don't know whether I am an efficient or a deficient minister, but I do recall something of which I will always be proud. The first thing I did was to close down completely an office called the Office of the Prime Minister, when I found out it answered no need whatsoever. Its place was taken by a small office where letters are answered, where a series of elementary things are attended to. This office has a very small staff. If we had followed the bureaucratic concept, we could have asked for the largest building and drawn up the largest of all organograms: a line here saying INDUSTRIES, a line there saying AGRICULTURE and another saying EDUCATION.

"Everyone knows, for example, all that education has done throughout the country, and how it was done. And to spark off all this activity, they did not require a building, nor a huge organogram, nor a ten or twelve million peso budget. And there you have the importance of concepts. Adhering to the old concept would have cost the republic eighty million pesos in eight years of revolution ... The capitalists had a lot of bureaucracy, and we have not eradicated it; we have, on occasion, increased it. There are factories, production units, where a capitalist owner employed three or four office employees, and we have twenty-five or forty. Why? We have to go to the root of the problem." (*Granma*, February 26, 1967.)

The root of the problem is bureaucracy, and the Cuban cure for bureaucracy is to end the division of labour and create the worker-intellectual. The worker-student programme will no doubt be facilitated by automation which cuts down the hours and harshness of labour so workers won't be too tired to study.

But is Fidel going to have to push the programme through almost single-handed? He set up a committee to cut down bureaucracy and soon had to denounce it for becoming bureaucratic. Cuba is full of die-hard bureaucratic élitists who believe in the division of labour. They continue, for example, to treasure chauffeurs. At the OLAS conference in Havana somebody made all the chauffeurs dress up, to lend dignity to the occasion. How do these relics survive in a genuine revolution?

In fact it is extraordinarily difficult to spot and actually pin down a bureaucrat; difficult even to define completely what bureaucrats are, except as lumps of inertia that plague all societies and bring revolution to a standstill. But the inertia's expertly disguised. Is a bureaucrat, for example, the sort of person Chaucer described:

> *A man so busy as he nowhere there nas,*
> *And yet he seemed busier than he was.*

Are they emotionally retarded people, generals who play at war as gravely as they used to play with toy soldiers? Were most of the people I met in the Cuban ministries bureaucrats? One man, thinking I was a guest of the Cuban Government, offered me his car to meet my wife at the airport, told me about his unpublished novel, asked was I happy, was I comfortable, did I want for anything — such total friendliness and humanity. I had to wait quite a long time for a pause in the courtesies to tell him that in fact I wasn't an invited guest — and he became almost savage. Within five seconds there was no car, no novel, nothing.

I was talking to a head of a government department about the shortage of matches and he wasn't making much sense, didn't seem desperately keen on explaining the shortage — then the phone rang, it was Fidel and he leapt to attention. Perhaps the ruling passion of bureaucrats is comfort, but in order to eat and pay rent and be generally comfortable they have to pretend to be involved and active; they are experts at disguise, like lizards, so you can't destroy them.

A fear of bureaucracy partly explains Fidel's ambivalent attitude to the communist party which he often regards as the great red hope of Cuban democracy, but occasionally cold-shoulders.

The plan of the party is that workers on factory and farm will elect representatives who, in turn, elect delegates to regional, provincial, and finally national councils, culminating in the Central Committee of the Communist Party and the politburo. At present party members are nominated by workers and finally selected by the party. Fidel spoke approvingly about the growing power of the party in January 1967: " . . . Other comrades should also speak at these rallies. One time Fidel, another Raul, another day Comrade Dorticos . . . the Central Committee in a word, as all of you say. And the time should come when we begin to change our slogans. Instead of saying 'Everyone with Fidel', rather 'Everyone with the Party'. We should begin to accustom ourselves to these changes and nothing should be more important to us."

It may be that an elected party will at some stage emerge in Cuba, just as the constitution now being worked on by Blas Roca, an old communist, may one day materialize; but the fact is that Castro not only wants to retain power in his own hands, but has a rooted distrust of saddling the Cuban people with a Soviet-style party bureaucracy — representatives entrenched in privileges, offering more and more "guidance" while doing less and less work, setting a bad example to workers; a host of multiplying middlemen between the plan and its performance, so that work is seen once again as a curse, needing special rewards and incentives to make it bearable.

Fidel expressed some of this discomfort about the bureaucracy of the Soviet bloc in his speech on Czechoslovakia: "Those who have visited [some of those socialist] countries, including the Cuban scholarship students, have often come back completely dissatisfied and displeased, and have said to us: 'Over there the youth are not being educated in the ideal of communism and the principles of internationalism; the youth there are highly influenced by all the ideas and tastes prevalent in the countries of Western Europe. In many places the main topic of conversation is money and incentives ... Some have told us in amazement, there is no such thing as volunteer work ... It is considered there that true volunteer work is almost an anti-marxist heresy. All sorts of things are done, even to such a point where the degree of skill in landing an aeroplane or making a parachute jump determines the granting of one kind of incentive or another. The sensibilities of many of our men have been injured by such vulgar use of material incentives or such vulgar commercialization of the conscience of men."

Fidel sees the danger that the Cuban communist party could easily come to reflect the policies, and sooner or later the will, of those other bureaucrats in Moscow. Fidel's rage against such "submissive, servile, tamed spirits" recently resulted in the sentencing of a party-member, Anibal Escalante, to fifteen years, and the indefinite postponement of the first congress of the party (Partido Communista de Cuba — PCC) which should have been held in 1967. Escalante was a long-time Cuban Stalinist, secretary-general of the old PSP (Partido Socialista Popular), who Fidel turned to in 1960-61 when he was desperate for guidance. It is due to Escalante that in many a semi-literate worker's room all over Cuba you can find tomes of Marx and Lenin. Cuban workers, he reasoned, were of low-political level; they ought to study *Capital*. As a result of this, and of other policies, such as putting cronies of high-political level in office, he became unpopular. People clapped in front of their television sets when Fidel denounced him in 1962.

This kind of public denunciation on television is harsh, and may even have been a cowardly way of making Escalante a scapegoat for the agonizing confusion in the economy, but at the same time Fidel likes to bring the people into everything and no doubt the public execution of a bureaucrat concentrates the mind of other bureaucrats wonderfully. Escalante went off to Prague and returned in 1964. He was put in charge of a State chicken farm and from this roost pushed the Soviet line in Cuba — the use of individual rather than collective incentives, lower investment, higher consumption, some reliance on profit motive and the free market, the abandonment of Che's revolution in Latin America, and the supremacy of the communist party. There is some evidence that the Russians were being tough in pressing this line to the point of threatening Fidel by cutting down on vital oil supplies. In announcing the oil cuts on January 2, 1968, Castro blandly absolved the Russians from all blame, but at the same time *Granma* devoted a quarter page to a simple account of how many million barrels of oil a day the Soviet Union produced. Every Cuban got the message.

In the same way, when Escalante was charged in January 1968 with activities amounting to counter-revolution, and sentenced to fifteen years, Raul Castro blamed the Russians by publicly absolving them of blame — pointing out that the Russian diplomat who had been dismissed for dealings with Escalante was absolutely untypical. Cubans assumed that the Russians were bent on subordinating Fidel to the Russian line, and to opportunists like Escalante. So Escalante was jailed to bring home to the Russians that Fidel wasn't manageable, and that Cuba wasn't going to adopt a reformist line that would mean the end of revolution both in Cuba and Latin America.

The rationing of petrol (gasolene), which hit the Cuban consumer harder than any previous measure since it cut off not only trips to the beach but trips to the country to buy blackmarket food, was brought home to the public as a result of Russian interference with oil supplies. To underline even more serious fears, "Oriente province celebrated Giron month [April 1968] with an unprecedented mobilization . . . to test plans for wartime. Tractors and trucks were replaced by ox-drawn ploughs and wagons; the use of all fuel-burning machinery or vehicles was eliminated. We will . . . have the most accurate idea possible of what we can produce in case of necessity, without a drop, or with a minimum, of fuel." (Raul Castro, May Day, 1968.) On March 13, 1968, Fidel, in a speech explaining shortages, linked petrol, Escalante and the Russians: "In part [complaints] have a real basis in real difficulties, and in part they may be related to such circumstances, as for example, the international relations of our party and government. It is possible that the need to ration gasoline and the circumstances surrounding the Central Committee meeting in which the pseudo-revolutionary currents, the microfactional elements were severely judged, have been factors that contributed to disquiet and uncertainty." In other words hard times were due both to genuine economic failures and to Soviet economic intrigue which involved Escalante and led to petrol rationing.

In their book *Socialism in Cuba* (Monthly Review Press, 1969) Huberman and Sweezy, distinguished socialists who support the Cuban revolution, nonetheless see the gaoling of Escalante as "a massive political fact that cannot be ignored", and "a sign of worsening relations between people and Government . . . Daily life is hard, and after ten years many people are getting tired. But there is more to it than that. The revolutionary leadership has made too many optimistic predictions that failed to materialize, too many promises that could not be kept. That these predictions and promises were honestly made, and reflected an underestimate of the difficulties to be overcome rather than an intent to deceive the people is an important fact; but it does little to alter the consequences. People are not only getting tired; they are tending to lose their faith, their confidence in the leadership's ability to keep its word. The ties that bind the masses to their paternalistic Government are beginning to erode.

"The leadership shows by its actions that it is aware of this situation. But it seems to reason that the erosion is as yet localized in certain geographical and social regions — principally the intellectuals and professionals and functionaries of the capital city. It apparently draws the conclusion that the first necessity is to shut these people up before they infect the rest of the population. After that the leadership counts on a sharp economic improvement to come to the rescue. When that happens the ties between government and people will be mended and there will no longer be need for harsh measures such as those against the microfaction.

"Perhaps it will work out that way. We hope so. But if it doesn't, if there are still quite a few years of austerity and deprivation ahead, there is a grave danger that the ties between people and government will continue to erode, and that the diabolic logic of the process will lead the government deeper and deeper into the ways of repression."

This is the familiar ghost, and one value of the Cuban revolution would be to lay it. If Castro wanted to silence the intellectuals in January 1968 he didn't succeed, because in 1968 there was open controversy in Cuba about the publication of a book of poems, *Outside the Game*, by Heberto Padilla, and a play *Seven Against Thebes*. The works were published with two conflicting introductions, the first by Cuban writers of the Cuban Artists and Writers Guild (UNEAC), disapproving of them but defending the freedom to write and publish; the second by members of the UNEAC international jury, who awarded prizes to the works and defended them most strongly. The general position taken by Cuban artists is that they are against both ivory tower art and dogmatic criticism of it. The dogmatists seem to be winning, for the moment at any rate. Padilla wasn't allowed to make the trip abroad which was part of his prize, and he subsequently lost his job at *Granma*. In 1969 the UNEAC jury consisted only of Cuban writers. There is clearly repression, raging controversy and defiance, but none of the silence of real fear.

The charges against the Escalante group were: "Attacks, by means of intrigues, against the principal measures of the revolution;

the distribution of clandestine propaganda against the line of the party; an attempt to proffer distorted orientation to several nuclei of the party; the presenting of false calumnious data about the plans of the revolution to officials of foreign countries with the intent of undermining the international relation of Cuba with other governments; the taking of secret documents from the Central Committee and the Ministry of Basic Industry; and the proselytizing and furthering of ideological divergences among certain militants who came from the ranks of the PSP ... It is also important to point out that the individuals who committed these crimes against the revolution do not at present hold any positions of leadership in the party. They constitute only nine party members and a few dozen resentful and opportunistic individuals who are unknown to the people and have nothing to do with the great tasks and plans of the revolution ... The political importance of these actions stems from the following circumstances: the microfaction came to coincide with arguments used and positions adopted against our revolution by Latin American pseudo-revolutionaries and the United States Central Intelligence Agency."

The jargon reads like a hangover from the Moscow trials (particularly because while one is used to a bank robbery being described and treated as criminal, one isn't used to thinking in those terms about a political line, even though it might change the course of a revolution, and affect the destinies of millions of people. Gaols full of thieves are far more acceptable than gaols full of political prisoners). It is unlikely however that the Escalante trial is the beginning of a Stalinist purge. Huberman and Sweezy inexplicably take at face value Raul's exoneration of the Russians, though they are as far as I know the only commentators to do so. The *New York Times*, for example, wrote on February 3, 1968: "The sentences, while not severe by Cuban standards, left no doubt that the Castro regime was setting an example through Mr Escalante of what happens to members of the revolutionary structure who seek support in the Soviet-led communist world to oppose Mr Castro.

"The affair ... also served as a warning to the Soviet Union not to meddle in Cuba's internal politics despite Cuba's dependence on the Soviet Union."

Once the Soviet rôle is accepted as crucial, then another reading of the affair seems to be that threatened with oil-cuts and an almost total disruption of the economy, Fidel rounded up forty people whom the Russians would use if they succeeded in overthrowing him. One, a chronic offender, was sentenced to fifteen years, eight to twelve years and all were expelled from the party. By dealing severely with Escalante, Fidel was making clear to the intellectuals and the people, as discreetly as he could, the grave situation with Russia. The Russians, like the CIA, were spreading hardship because Fidel's methods, particularly his revolutionary stance in Latin America, didn't suit them. Revolutions close ranks because of attack and are attacked because they close ranks.

Heberto Padilla's *Outside the Game*, a book of sad bitchy poems, includes one called "Instructions for entering a new society":

> *The first thing: you must be*
> *optimistic.*
> *The second: neat, restrained and obedient*
> *(you should have passed all the tests in sports).*
> *And finally walk*
> *like every member:*
> *one step ahead, and*
> *two or three backwards:*
> *but always applauding.*

A member of the Central Committee of the Party told me, "All in all, we are having unbelievable economic success which can't be long disguised from the rest of the world. Fidel, miraculously, is unchallenged. Why don't we complete the picture? Why do we round up and question and send home a few students who do a little demo about Czechoslovakia? All we do is disguise how tiny they are. Cuban students aren't angry against the Government. So why don't we let the few march? And why do we shut down little magazines? It's the work of a few Mayor Daleys who want to get their hands on people. All this little piddling repression is not Fidel's style, but he can't see to everything. You know Fidel's dictum is 'within the revolution, everything; outside the revolution, nothing'. Little poems and magazines are within the revolution. So are demonstrations about Czechoslovakia."

The struggle of the Soviet Union to control Cuba has, so far as one can judge, ended in Soviet defeat. Fidel's domestic policy remains unchanged. Various Cubans told me that he has temporarily shifted his Latin American policy closer to the Russian because he has no alternative; and also because he calculates that to make Cuba an economic show-case will be some incentive to Latin American revolution. For the next five or ten years, they say, he will make Cuba rich and lessen his dependence on the Soviet Union by European trade, then he will go back to supporting revolutionaries. In the meantime the Latin American sore will have conveniently festered and he himself will still be only fifty or so, ready to treat it.

If this is true, it is the kind of opportunism that will delight reactionaries, disgust revolutionaries, and get Fidel execration from both sides. How would a Cuban show-case help revolution in Latin America? Latin American revolutionaries aren't troubled so much by doubts about revolution as by bullets made in the United States. Perhaps — who knows — full shops in Cuba will impress the United States with the wisdom of revolution, and the wolf will finally graze with the lamb. Douglas Bravo, the Venezuelan revolutionary, has recently (January 1970) denounced Fidel, his old ally, as a Russian satellite, but that may only mean that Fidel has now switched to supporting his rivals. At the end of 1969 Brazilian revolutionaries were still accepting invitations to Havana (*Granma*, October 5, 1969).

After my visit to the CDR meeting I spent some days casing that particular block, asking questions about personal liberty.

"We eat. We work. It's the same old life. But don't talk to me, talk to my children. They say it's different." This was from a half-literate woman who had six children. The eldest son was a doctor, his graduation photograph on the wall. A daughter was about to qualify in mechanical engineering, a younger daughter had just started a medical course, one son was in an army school, the two youngest boys were in high school. She sneakingly felt that with all that achievement she ought to be living in a big house, and here she was in a tenement. What was the good?

One daughter bubbled in, the mechanical engineer. She was muddy. She chatted, waiting to get into a shower which they shared with about twelve neighbours. She'd been doing voluntary work in the fields.

"How many hours?"

"Oh, a few."

"Don't you watch the clock?"

She laughed. All the people she'd been responsible for had turned out, she said. Her mother was preparing the spaghetti. There was something else in another pan, but I couldn't see what. The work wasn't all that efficient, the daughter said, but at least it wouldn't have to be done all over again.

She turned on the radio and jigged to the Argentine pop-idol Leonardo Farvio. She came back to talking about the work. She seemed to yearn for efficiency. Voluntary labour was low-productive, she said, and hand-work was too slow. Mechanical engineers like herself must invent machines. She laughed, patting herself on the back. There were too many girls thinking about men, she said. Machines were more reliable, no?

Did she have a boyfriend? Yes, of course. Her mother sighed, and I changed the subject. I wanted to know whether she thought low production might come from lack of material incentives and the freedom to buy all the little things people like. I pointed out, for example, that in spite of machinery, agricultural production in the Soviet Union was still low. Yes, yes, she said, sometimes they produce about one-twentieth of the US with similar equipment and know-how. Sometimes it was as bad as that. But they have problems.

"What problems?"

"Well, they're like our parents," she laughed. "They work only to buy goods, and if they can't buy goods they don't work, and if they don't work there are no goods to buy. Especially as they all have to pretty well share whatever there is, unlike the good old US where a third of the people starve. Some problem." A confident girl, almost swaggering, rolling at least in the freedom of literacy, in the liberty of ideas. I said: "Where do you get your facts about the US?"

"From *Granma*. They're correct, no?"

"No."

"Well anyway, let's say there is very great inequality, and millions very poor."

"Yes, but Cuban equality is a luxury largely paid for by Russia, so much so the Russians can't afford another revolution in a Latin American country, especially a large one."

"How do you mean?"

"Well, the free hospitals, schools — Cubans don't produce enough to pay for those."

She went so silent her mother looked up from the second pot, which I now saw had minced meat in it.

"The facts," the girl said after a moment, "are the following: our main product is sugar which has seldom fallen below five million tons, and in 1970 will be ten million tons — although we suffered three years of severe drought which destroys sugar-cane, drastic reorganization of the industry, and primitive conditions like cutting cane by hand. Moreover there were substantial advances in cattle, citrus, rice, coffee, and the building of dams for irrigation."

I wondered whether this picture wasn't too optimistic. I pointed out that although Fidel had announced, for example, that the rice crop had tripled in 1968 it was still only 50,000 tons, whereas in 1960 rice production was 323,000 tons. As a result Cubans had little rice to eat. She said: "We cut back on rice production because we had no technicians and were producing inefficiently. We wanted to plant scientifically on a vast scale with the right land, and proper facilities and equipment. It took us years to do the research and train the technicians. Because of the blockade we had to steal good varieties of rice from the Philippines. Now we are well away, ahead of schedule in fact, and by 1971 we'll have a *surplus* of over half a million tons, that is after feeding our eight and a half million people all the rice they need. To feed all the people you need technology. Of course you can have technology like the Yankees and dump the stuff. The *New York Times* and such papers seldom explain any of the difficulties we face. They merely say that rice production has fallen in Cuba, implying that communism doesn't work, and that our agriculture is bound to lag, like the Soviet Union's. That's your free press. They should explain that during the long years of US domination Cuba remained backward. We knew how to dance and to go to the beach and book a ticket for the US, but we knew nothing. But even so, in ten years, five of them full of elementary mistakes that an educated people wouldn't have made, Cuba has turned herself from an illiterate colony into a more or less advanced nation, producing ten million tons of sugar, exporting food to pay for aid. The reason the lines are so long is that we export food to pay our debts. The Russian debt was large, and some of it will have to be written off, but recently our exports have begun to match our imports, so that in a few short years Cuba will be very nearly self-supporting."

I said that the Russian debt was in fact growing. I couldn't quote the figure (174·6 million rubles in 1966, 220 million in 1969) but she said she accepted the fact, "because of the expensive investments particularly in sugar. But these investments are at last beginning to pay off, particularly with the coming [ten-million-ton] harvest."

"Are they wise investments?"

"Yes, obviously."

She had clearly pored over *Granma*, studied it avidly, absorbed it, but *Granma* probably hasn't reported that there are differences of opinion among Cuban economists about producing ten million tons of sugar. And why not report it? Why shouldn't questions like this be discussed publicly so that intelligent Cubans can be in the picture? Would they work with less heart to get the ten million tons or would they, seeing the pros and cons weighed and understanding the decision to go ahead, feel more responsible and work harder? Ought not a revolutionary newspaper to be more democratic and set itself far higher standards of truth than a bourgeois press which often has to think of its advertisers? Castro is so justifiably popular that the Cuban press can even afford to discuss issues fully.

I told her that there was a line of thinking among Cuban economists that the ten-million-ton harvest was a Castro spectacular totally unjustified by economic calculation. Their argument was that to produce eight and a half million tons would only need an investment of 300 million pesos, whereas to produce ten million tons would need an investment of over one billion pesos. In other words the last one and a half million tons would be wildly uneconomical. She brushed this aside. "Ten million tons," she said, " is a real challenge for the revolution and the enthusiasm aroused throughout the country — well, can't you see it? It is priceless. That kind of enthusiasm can even be turned into money. How can you separate political from economic calculation? It is political awareness that produces wealth. Fidel has to teach this to our economic bureaucrats. Left to them we'd go bankrupt worrying about dollars and cents."

Russian aid, she said, could easily have fallen into the hands of people like this. Aid was vital, but also vital was the way it was used. Cuba had made, at great sacrifice, a huge capital investment that was now beginning to pay off. Not one private motor car had been imported since the revolution. Russian aid could easily have underwritten a corrupt, inefficient bureaucracy with an expensive Soviet-dominated army to defend its interests. A communist backwater in the Caribbean.

Her articulateness was the revolution's best witness. Where did she get it from? Due to a lack of experienced teachers the education in the schools is still mostly indifferent (though a UN expert told me he thought the TV education, in quality and quantity, as good as any in the world). The newspapers are usually ponderous, written in lead. I think her articulateness comes from being brought up on

Fidel's speeches which, rhetoric aside, often state problems suc-
cinctly — very direct, very clear, no jargon, full of definitions, facts
and figures. Dull Cubans merely repeat the ideas. Bright Cubans
pick up the method and the confidence. There are thousands of
Cubans like this girl, light years away from their parents. This is
more than social mobility; it is mass migration of a whole generation
from one level of civilization to another. Her Jamaican equivalent
would be an ignorant servant.

They were ready to eat and the mother had no intention of inviting
me, but the girl did. She'd shower and then we'd eat, then she had
to meet her boyfriend. I wasn't staying to eat, in spite of dying to
talk more to the girl, and tried to make a date with her and her
boyfriend for the following evening in my hotel to eat a meal. She
refused. She seemed to feel a sort of fastidious recoil from the idea
of "dining out", as though it were a vulgar and pointless thing to do.
Then she asked: "You will say in your book there is no freedom in
Cuba?"

"I won't say that, no, I certainly won't say that."

"But less freedom than the United States?"

"In one important sense, that their press can fully criticize the
Government. Yours can't. I realize that they have more to criticize,
but you should understand that it is partly because they allow
criticism that demonstrations rock the Government."

"They rock Johnson," she said, "and get Nixon."

"No, those demonstrations and riots rock the system."

"But not because the people in the ghettoes read the *New York
Times*?"

"Because they hear about Malcolm X, and see what their
Government does in Vietnam. The most brutal, large-scale mas-
sacres could happen and people not know, if the press didn't choose
or wasn't there to report it. Malcolm X would have found it more
difficult to become a national figure without the capitalist press.
And he rocks that system."

"So we, in turn, must sell *Time* magazine? What kind of comparison is this people make? Look at the damage socialist countries

have suffered in the last fifty years from capitalism. On the other hand, what damage has capitalism sustained from us? What blood have they lost? In the US socialism is a paper enemy, a theory. They have shelves full of books about it. Students flirt happily with it in their youth. For us capitalism is a grave. The Soviet Union had millions of dead less than thirty years ago. So did our Chinese comrades. Cubans fell at Giron. Capitalism is death for us and we won't have *Time* magazine, not because it might influence us but because it offends us."

She was angry, but civil. Her look implied that she hoped my book wouldn't propagate capitalism. She said: "Even our own press is not for criticism. We have other channels for that. Our press simply makes up for the books we lack. There are long articles full of information which you, perhaps, consider biased because they don't say there are two sides to every question."

"Why have you gone hostile?"

"Oh, there's no arguing with those vested interests. So you send me your book, and I'll send you a gun."

She went to check on the shower, saying: "When we work only three days a week and eat well, then they'll stop worrying about freedom. They're materialists. But a three-day week will never come. Too many starving people need our help. Think," she said, "if the rest of the third world got aid and used it like Cuba, the world's food and literacy problem would already be solved. As it is in China with Soviet aid. Instead of helping, the US blockade us and bomb Vietnam."

The block was shabby, overcrowded, two or three to a room, the rooms kept clean by mothers and grannies who had been poor all their lives but impervious to politics, holding on to their poverty because for them the only alternative to bad is worse. Left to them Fidel would still be slaying mosquitoes in the Oriente bush. Their normal self-interest has been crippled by propaganda and fear. Like Che's Bolivian Indians, they are "impenetrable as stones". In Latin America revolutionaries have nearly always ended on the gallows.

As a result young Cubans believe that the foundation of liberty is political awareness, and call elections held without this awareness the "electoral farce".

A few days later I ran into a hurricane named Mrs S, a wiry, untidy woman with a bitter mouth although her eyes had a brightness which might have been amusement. The famous Cuban literacy, she stormed, was indoctrination. There was no dissent. Literacy wasn't everything. Dr Goebbels was a Ph.d. It was like a new dark age in Cuba. The New York and London *Times* were there in the National Library and the students were so brainwashed they never read them. She had lectured in the States and was now ill and ageing. "And anyway, can't you see that it is better to be illiterate and poor than spied on? They know who visits me and who I visit. My God, can you believe it? And if any crisis comes I'm marked for jail. Under Mr Castro it's suddenly my neighbour's duty to know how I live. Everybody knows that in any civilized country your neighbours are your natural enemies. Your house is a fortress. Here in Cuba every jackass is knocking on your door to give you advice about who you should see and who is dangerous. And if you say go to hell, they feel righteous.

"You tell me this happens in all countries where there is danger of attack, but this thing is inherent in communism. It is happening to Russia and again now in China. Communism wants to destroy man's indestructible sense of territory, clean up the jungle. They want to take the lock off my front door. You say, I don't have to go to their eternal meetings, but then I feel disapproved of. I sit here groaning, feeling I'm a public enemy. I can't leave. I'm a Cuban. I have no family to go to. I can see you sitting there, thinking I'm a *gusano* and that I exaggerate. Well, you don't live here. At first I went out into the fields, I stood guard. People, people, people. Even after you lock your door and sit alone by the radio, you dread it won't be for long. And what for? So everybody on the continent can eat and have a room? But if everybody has it, who wants it? People only desperately want what they don't have. Don't they understand that? Our deepest need is to be on our own, different, non-conformist. To avoid other people, no matter how virtuous they are. To laugh at them, hate them, have defences against them. I am as much a fighter for independence as Fidel Castro. My motto is 'Leave people alone' — to be crooks, exploiters, saints, torturers, anything that satisfies their private needs which no man can measure. Compared with this, literacy, food, hospitals are nothing. You said just now, why don't I just do the minimum and everybody would accept that. I could lock my door in peace. Well, why don't I? I agree there are several people on the block who do the minimum, or even do nothing, and seem quite happy. Everybody knows that they like Fidel, even if they are a bit lazy. Everybody knows who visits them but nobody cares very much. I suppose that's true. They don't complain of interference. If a crisis comes they won't be arrested. But what sort of people are they? Grey people, weak people, not like me. They could live under stones. The world is full of obedient little people, but they'll never invent anything. Inventors are people basically disobedient; opposed to any *status quo*. Their instinct is to be different. This is the whole principle of invention and freedom — to see things differently. This is what democracies enshrine.

"In capitalism," she said, "you expect men to be devils. They sometimes aren't but you expect devilry and self-interest and that is a sensible basis on which to live. You expect ambition, privilege, inequality, so you legislate on a *laisser-faire* basis, only making sure that extremes don't get too impossible. In communism ordinary men are supposed to be angels, so you end up with a lot of cynicism and pretence, with a lot of nasty flies winging about like angels, blind to their privileges. Communists try to do too much. They don't understand people. Don't you know that the more equal men get, the more watchful they are about any trace of privileges? And of course there is bound to be privilege so the greater the equality the more the misery. Life is like that. No movements can contain it. It over-runs all movements.

"In capitalism you have separate principalities and powers, various places for people to hide, hundreds of different currents and directions. You can find ways, for example, of not working: as a hippie, a pimp, a crook, a gigolo, a university professor. It is intolerable to have one power in the state, even a righteous power, because human beings have a perverse desire to say no, even to righteousness. To disagree. They need at least the illusion of freedom.

"Really, these fools want to abolish money when money introduces the only equality. Everybody is in a sordid chase for sordid money and there is no particular righteousness about those who get it. It is a great equalizer. And it perfectly symbolizes the futility of life. It is something unimportant that we pretend is important. It buys goods that delight us for a time but less and less, and it can't buy happiness. We put it at the centre of society as a kind of decoy because we know there are more important things hidden somewhere.

"And again money symbolizes our true attitude to people. We have neutral commercial money relations with most people, and those who are near to us we exploit. Money sums it all up. It is a perfect love substitute. You pursue it to be free from the intolerable love of people.

"In capitalism money and laws are the centre, not people. You make impersonal laws to be carried out impersonally by paid judges and policemen. It's their job, that's all, no preaching at you. Vice is taken for granted so you set up jails, hang men, declare war. Communism has failed again and again in history. It tried to take over Christianity and failed."

When I next met the medical student I read him my notes on Mrs S and asked what he thought. His answer was that she seemed to be saying that since there was no justice in life, you shouldn't try to make it as just as possible.

"I wonder if it's philosophers like her who sit in the Pentagon and drop bombs on us, without fear of retaliation. It's a nice position to be in."

I said to him: "Do you feel any privacy on this block?"

"Well, everybody knows what you do, but you aren't part of a big horrible family; you do what you like. That lady says what she likes but she still eats, has a job."

I explained that she had lost her job as a teacher long ago, but went on being paid. The Government had suggested one or two other jobs, such as translating, but she was in fact too ill to do anything. The neighbour who shopped for her had told me that the reason she was so dotty about privacy was to hide the fact that she never had a man.

The medical student said: "People can do anything they like. They can make blue movies if they have the camera and film. In this block I do what I like, and we all know who are the self-appointed spies. Go and talk to Mrs Blanco."

I came to Cuba, my ears buzzing with accounts of the new anti-semitism in Eastern Europe and the new Stalinism in Russia — the informers, the hush-hush, the sudden executions, the new czars in curtained limousines, the waitresses whose order-pads concealed listening devices. These stories come echoing from communist regimes that sound like regions of hell, and hit dark nerves in my belly. The sudden executions seem far more terrible than the sudden executions in the US. I believe in my head that more people are shot down in the States for political, racial and other criminal reasons, than in the Soviet Union. But I don't believe it in my belly. The dead men in the East are more dead. I found young Cubans again and again incredulous that a black man like me didn't realize that Siberia was no worse than the black ghettoes, no less a life-sentence, and the misery and death-rate probably lower. Russian jails, they said, are no worse than Nixon's, which are full of black rebels like Malcolm X and Eldridge Cleaver. I reel at the idea of Nixon's jails. No of course not. One talks of Stalin's jails but not of Nixon's jails. Nixon has no jails. And Nixon's elected.

We have only one morning paper in Jamaica — the *Daily Gleaner* — so that Jamaicans tend to call all newspapers *Gleaners*. Jamaica's population is one and a half million. Most of us emigrate. We go to London and ask the man for a *Gleaner* and the man, knowing the score by now, hands us an *Express* or an *Evening News* — same political complexion.

Darkness at Noon was, I think, serialized in the *Daily Gleaner* when I was a child. Or perhaps it was another book called *Out of the Night*. Anyway, it marked me for life. My mother as well. When she wrote me a letter about Cuba she was afraid actually to mention the place by name. She called it "that foreign country".

I visited Mrs Blanco wanting to find out how much power she had, and she caught on almost at once that I'd been told she was an informer. She cut right in.

"Yes, I know what everybody says about me, but I have to see to it that people don't do certain things, like being absent from work. No absenteeism on this block. I am supposed to be dealing with children absent from school, but I passed this man, who used to be a good man, but something is happening; too much bartering, and a little gambling I believe somewhere."

"But no, he was always like that," her husband said. She was impatient.

"Yes, I know. I was beating round the bush for this gentleman's benefit. In fact the man has a girlfriend in Marianao and can only see her in the day when he's supposed to be at work, so he's claiming sickness and toothache and even stress — I don't know where he found that word — what is stress? What does he know about stress? I felt like following him one day and catching him out, because after all it *is* my business. He is a parasite letting down my block. But I talked to the comrades and they say this would only drive him away from the revolution. The wife of course doesn't know the half. She's out at work. He lets her carry the children to the nursery and bring them home and do the housework, while he goes out with the girlfriend. Cuban men! So I'm supposed to be dealing with absentee children — I check with the teacher then check with the parents — but this man sticks in my crop so I say one word to him, in front of his wife. I say to him: 'What is this *stress*?' and he knows I know and he's frightened. I didn't think we would have any more stress, and he was all right for two days.

I checked with his work people. Two days. Then more stress. He was desperate for this girlfriend, and had to see her in the days, because her husband comes home at nights — you see there are not too many whore-houses in Havana nowadays, but these Cuban men are goats, so now they have girlfriends, usually married, so I wondered if I shouldn't talk to the girlfriend and I put it to the comrades, but they said no, I must stick to absentee children. But what is anybody doing about this man? The block is suffering. In Batista's days a man like this would leave his work if his prick tickled him and his poor wife and children would starve. In this revolution women are not at the mercy of men. The wife works, the children go to the nursery, they get clothes, they get food. You know what anxiety that woman would have in Batista's day? She would be murdering the children because they were bawling for food. She would be lying on her bed with anxiety, getting cold and fever. She would get up before day and just walk all about, all about, not seeing, not hearing, and come back home and the next room would be shouting at her about going out and leaving the children to bawl. Then a non-stop quarrel for days, blows and probably hospital. But this is revolution, and that blasted man must work. So the Committee say I must leave him alone to his conscience and his work-mates, but they don't seem to be doing anything. I don't want to get a name for interfering."

"That," said the husband, "is the worst kind of name."

"They think I'm interfering," she went on, "so I'm not saying anything, but I'm watching from here what is happening. I'm watching. Thank God the wife is healthy and well, but what a pain if she finds out about him."

"Pshaw," said the husband, "that is a common thing."

I asked her where the absentee lived. She showed slight panic and hesitation, but her husband told me.

In the corner of Mrs Blanco's kitchen a child of about fifteen had been fiddling with a radio for the news. Statistics about malnutrition in Latin America. Great interest. People like this in Jamaica would be listening to statistics about the Kingdom of Heaven. Brother W, our local Jesus Christ, is one of thousands of North Americans who make their living saving souls in the Caribbean and Latin America. And nowadays a hefty part of the salvation message is anti-communism. I discovered that my nephew, who lives in Jamaica and earns £5 a week, gave £40 to one mission. The receipts came to the house and his mother, who has to work till midnight making ends meet, couldn't believe it. "Forty pounds," she kept saying, "forty pounds, and he not paying me rent or food!"

My nephew believes that heaven is somewhere among white people in the United States. There is a lot of lunacy in the Caribbean. I grew up singing:

> *Nothing to pay no*
> *Nothing to pay*
> *Jesus has died to*
> *Open the way*
> *Free is the ticket, starting today*
> *Kingston to heaven, and nothing to pay.*

The light of Christ and Brother W shines in every hovel in the Caribbean, outside Cuba, and is the not-so-secret weapon of capitalism in the area. The CIA is nothing compared to it. People in these parts have never heard of Russia, but they know all about Satan, and communism is anti-Christ. It would need an enormous operation to change this, and all the means of propaganda are in the hands of capitalism. This is why the Cubans insist that in Latin America bullets are the fundamental road to power.

The absentee and his wife were watching television drama, an incredible business of slapped faces that snapped back defiant, chained hands, and blazing revolutionary eyes. Her head was in his comfortable lap. They offered to turn down the telly, but I said I'd come again. The comfort seemed unbreakable.

I managed to see him two weeks later. He was still happily loafing, taking two or three days off a week. Since there's little to buy, many Cubans can live on half a month's wages, so absenteeism is a serious problem in Cuba and the subject of many a government campaign. A report published in *Granma*, for example (October 1969), made clear that on one farm in Camaguey attendance was as low as forty-five per cent, and in most places no higher than sixty-five per cent. "During the months of May, June and July work attendance of the agricultural workers did not go higher than sixty-five per cent, and they averaged six hours per man daily. During the month of September, when we really began to lead and take care of the workers, work attendance went up to eighty per cent, and hours-per-man rate reached seven-point-nine. Of course we are just beginning."

Taking care of the workers still means small things like making refreshments available to them. Large scale improvements like better housing will have to wait many years. But the Government is avoiding repression. Published in *Granma* for every absentee to read is a chastisement of those managers who simply want to transfer absentees, and the argument that absenteeism is as much a reflection on the manager as it is on the absentee. Cuban production could probably be doubled if there was no absenteeism, and there is a desperate shortage of labour, yet Castro avoids even standard coersive devices like raising prices or lowering wages so that absentees would be forced to work harder to live. The revolutionary method is appeal to conscience. This most central problem of socialism, the problem of incentive, is to be solved neither by Stalinist repression, nor neo-capitalist devices, but by conscience. I wondered how this worked in practise; what actually happened in the factories.

"I don't get paid for the days I don't work," said Mrs Blanco's *bête noire*, "so no problem." Nobody on the block was saying anything, but at work they were "nagging and threatening and all that shit. They'll get fed up and send me to agriculture for a few months and that'll cure me, won't it?" We were in my hotel and the band was playing, *Yah, yah, yah, Delilah.* He started humming.

"What do they actually say to you at work?"

"They are very joky," he said, sarcastically. "They say 'Well, Comrade, in Havana you think about nothing but food. And where to find a little woman. You think of nothing else. Sex and rice. So agricultural work will be good. The clean open air. The country. You will fall in love with the country. Very exciting.' "

"What do you say?"

"Man, the last thing I want is to leave Havana. You know there's this woman I see. She's a staunch CDR lady on her block, but left to her I'd never get to work. She wants me every day, every day, but impossible. And night absolutely impossible — her husband, my wife. So every other day we ride 'em cowboy. All day."

"In her house?"

"No."

"Why? The CDR?"

"No, not so much the CDR; she's thick with the CDR. But she says her bed is for husband. If I want to be husband OK, if not *posada.*" (Posadas are houses which let rooms to couples who want a bed. They often queue up.)

"So we go to *posada*, and to one or two places we know, like one dark underground car park. Oh, if I go to agriculture she'll find another bastard like me and there would I be in agriculture ploughing for Castro. How could I stand it? I'll go to jail. I need my wife, I need this other bitch. The one thing I don't need is the job."

"What's the job?"

"Nothing. Sticking labels on bottles. Women can do that."

"How many people take days off?"

"Oh, it used to be a lot. Oh man, a lot. Now it's just a few."

"What made the change?"

"Oh they sent them off to the country to be somebody's problem. And I think a few went to prison, you know."

"For how long?"

"Oh I guess one, two years. So now it's only few. But I'm so young. I don't have enough women and I can't think of anything else. You know in films they show how they used to castrate guards in harems but the buggers could still do it, you know. And better still, the women wouldn't get pregnant. It was fiesta."

"Why don't you study if you don't like sticking labels?"

"I don't like studying. When the revolution came I was sixteen. Out of school. No steady job, left school at twelve. At nine really. Then revolution and they send me to school. I nearly finished junior high school. But I'm no good for studying. I married. Got a job. My wife too. And my mother. Everybody. We work, go to pictures. Eat at restaurants. We live like kings. I lose pay for not going to work but I earn all I need to live. So why work every day? Though if I were a rich man, I'd know what to do in Cuba." He meant black-marketing.

"What is the black-market position?"

"Well, I have no idea at all, of course, but can't you guess? You think before the revolution, Havana was one big black-market. In Batista days, on this block, everybody had one foot in a racket. The policeman next door was a merchant in Swiss watches. To keep a good police record he arrested his business rivals — the ones he didn't shoot. That's a fact. He was a Batista admirer. And my mother was dealing in marijuana, selling it to people, her sister beside her shouting to them it was wickedness, and my mother, her head down, folding a tiny square of the stuff. And all these people are still in Cuba — doing what, you think?"

He went to dance and the medical student who was with us, very drunk, started shouting to me over the music that he'd just had a horrid fantasy of a Cuba filled with black-marketeers, and absentees shot or sent to jail.

"And think, it isn't true! Cuba, by God, has made it!" he shouted to the bar full of Russian tourists. "This dago country has made it! It isn't, as the Yankee Schlesinger said, a mendicant communist satellite in the Caribbean." He turned and said softly to me: "You don't have to hold your breath and hope it isn't. It *isn't*. Cuba is about to produce ten million measurable tons of sugar. Or nine million. What does it matter? And I," he said sadly, looking at his hands, "cut some of it."

That was one of my memorable moments in Cuba. I had this sudden feeling of Cubans with held breath, silently watching their own revolution. The classic argument against socialism, of course, is that men work to buy things and to get ahead and that if you take those reasons away the only alternative is terror. That is why to die-hard capitalists Cuba must not succeed, or must be written off as too small to count, or as a special case. But Cuba so far *has* succeeded in its goal of bread without terror. The cane for the 1970 harvest was cut by 350,000 volunteers, some driven by conscience, some by herd-feeling, some by the camaraderie of the cane-fields, some by the excitement of the occasion; none by hunger or terror. (There were, *Granma* reports, far more volunteers than could be used.) Unfortunately many of these willing hearts have erratic work habits, and in November 1969 Fidel, giving them instructions for the harvest, appealed for discipline.

"It is of basic importance that a worker, once he has finished his work shift, turn over the machine under his care to the man who comes to relieve him — not when he meets his relief man at the entrance to the mill or in the bus, or on some street corner, but at his post. It is of fundamental importance that every worker feel responsible for the machine that he operates until his relief comes; he must give his relief man a detailed report, and he must not leave till his relief turns up. This in turn points up the importance of work discipline and attendance, and gives a clear idea of the consequences of absenteeism on the operation of the mills. The importance of work discipline must be emphasised at all times, always appealing to the workers' sense of responsibility. That is not a battle to be waged by administration or leaders; it is a battle to be taken up by all the people.

"Socialist society does not have coercive methods — the old standbys of unemployment, hunger, and the terrible consequences which a worker faced if he did not meet the obligations imposed by the capitalist. We no longer have lines of men waiting at the gates of the sugar mill — that is why the revolution which liberates man from these scourges, the revolution which works for all the people, depends, essentially, not on the will of its leaders — no! but on the will of the entire people, on what the workers themselves are capable of accomplishing. This does not mean that cadres holding positions of responsibility should not be demanding. To be demanding does not mean to threaten anyone or to punish anyone. It is true that in certain specific cases punishment must be applied, but this is not a question of punishment, nor can punishment be the remedy, because there is something essential in man, something far more powerful than any other stimulus, something that can achieve much more than hunger, the threat of unemployment or poverty ever did in the past, and this thing is man's sense of his own dignity. This is his stimulus — each man's feeling of self-esteem, his sense of honour, his sense of dignity, the importance he places on the opinion that others have of him — this is the stimulus that has led individuals and entire peoples to accomplish wonders. And it is most difficult, almost abnormal, to find a man who is absolutely lacking in dignity, in honour.

"We could say that the basic duty of those who lead is to know how to appeal to this trait in man. Substantial changes are often obtained in work centres through such appeals. Incredible changes have been brought about in many places."

"Of course Fidel can talk," said an ex-manager I talked to, out in the country. "He's like a school-teacher with a cane. He doesn't have to use it. He has it, and he tells you, 'Oh, it's easy, just coax them; look how quiet they are. How fucking still. It's beautiful. *You* get the same results.'

"Well, I didn't get the same results. In my factory we had a high loss in man days — sometimes half the place absent, sometimes thirty per cent, that is three out of ten. Of course, then the party rolls in with this guy in a bitch of a car, chauffeur, everything, even cigars to hand round, all the way from Havana, chats them up — these peasants, they gawp and there are no absences for a few days and he says 'See, just coax them. No brute force. You don't have to transfer them. It's not their fault. It's yours.' You hear that? *My* fault. Just a little firm coaxing. And when he phones a month later to check, two out of the usual three have gone absent again but he says, 'See, it's a great success. Thirty per cent success, with one visit. If I could be there all the time — one hundred per cent.' Now one of these poor fools he coaxed back dines out on this visit from the party in Havana. A more or less personal visit to him. What can you do with people like that? Can you follow what I'm telling you? The man from Havana leaves me in the shit with my people. They glance at me as if to say '*He* could get us back, but *you* couldn't.' So I packed the whole fucking thing in. Now I'm more or less a cow-hand after being factory manager. My God, oh my God. They keep on saying good management would cut down absenteeism, good managers like Fidel, yes, but do I have what he has, the cars, the cigars, all that overhead? The fucking army took over my factory. Good, very good. They'll coax one day and shoot the next. Between you and me, sometimes Fidel is a big fat fart of a big Daddy talking shit."

He wasn't really only a cow-hand, but clearly he was on the skids emotionally: "Fidel this, and Fidel that, and bloody Fidel will have to be dead before I get another job. Why was I born a bloody Cuban? Abroad if you get fucked up with one firm there are others. Here you are finished. Fidel is vengeful. You come here visiting, you know the bitterness people feel against that man?

"I am not a *gusano*, but what is before me now, but to leave Cuba? My friends tell me: 'Work your way back. Look at X, he worked back.' Fuck that, who is Fidel? I fought, he fought, so why isn't he begging me for a job? Luck. It's that last extra roll of the dice that makes the difference. If you hear the bullet sing you are alive, if you don't you're dead. And if there's free speech in Cuba, then I can say perhaps there's still a bullet marked Fidel, can't I? How I got the job? Oh, I was the buddy of a buddy — how do people get jobs in Cuba? A friend says to Fidel 'I know a man . . . ' Fidel says 'I'm tired of men, I want a genius. Preferably an Oriente peasant.' Like this bastard who's taken my job. This melon. No background. This black arse-hole known only to himself. And he's in charge. And then he'll get fired like me and want to shoot Fidel. That's Cuba. Land of mystery and women."

I talked to the new soldier/manager, a bright, newly educated Cuban, about thirty-five, black: a growing reputation in the province, one or two comforting clichés at his fingertips, not many more.

"What is your rank?"

"Does that matter? No, no, that doesn't really matter."

"Rank counts in the Cuban army."

"Yes, we inherited a lot of things from the Russians, but rank only makes sense in a class society. It can't last long in Cuba," he said, with some show of daring.

"Why is the army taking over farms and factories?"

"I suppose really because every revolutionary is a soldier. The army embodies the idealism of the Cuban people: to destroy exploitation and defend revolution. To make the mad-house world a little more bearable, as we've done here in Cuba. The dream of every Cuban child is to be a terrific soldier like Che and Camillo. All our heroes are soldiers. But when you say take over factories all it means is we are put in charge of civilians with no more authority than any civilian administrator. There is neither court-martial nor block-house."

"But why take over the farms and factories? The army smells of force and cows don't take orders."

"Nor even give them, which is a pity because our cow-hands would then know what to do. No, the position is that the army has such complicated weapons nowadays that our best soldiers have to be technicians. So they can double up very usefully in the farms and factories where we need technology. The man who drives a tank can drive a tractor. It's got nothing to do with giving or taking orders. The army at present has the most knowledgeable people around. Also some of the most revolutionary. As I said, the dream of every Cuban boy is to be Che. Not dream, determination. Dreams won't create the new man in America."

"Who is he? Describe him."

"New men with socialist natures."

"You feel you're a new man?"

"Well in the sense that I act on my ideals. That is the way I was brought up. I can fight. I can produce. My education was that of the new man. I am willing to go anywhere in Cuba to increase production and I don't ask how much they'll pay me."

"Aren't you jealous if a friend of yours gets a bigger factory to run?"

"I personally feel, thank God. Rather him than me. But I know comrades who would be jealous. And that's good. It's good to pine after the big job so long as you can pull it off."

"You don't feel jealousy is a vice?"

"It's a bible vice. People are going to be jealous, but so what? You can't restrain people's thoughts or feeling but only their actions. A good man does a good job, and doesn't bother with intrigue."

"My impression is that it isn't just naked absenteeism that's the problem, but also loafing."

"They're both problems. But you're right about the four-hour day. You only need one loafer in a team to destroy their rhythm and pace. He goes to the toilet, he decides to have a smoke, he talks in a way that amuses his mates, or he bores them but what can they do? They drop hints about fulfilling the quota and he agrees, but then forgets. Soon they're all working at his pace, telling their own stories. Soon the next bench are all doing the same thing. This sort of thing spreads like germs because, you see, people are only waiting for a chance to work at their natural pace which is quite slow. Much too leisurely, with a lot of talking. It's all right for a Sunday in the fields, this picnic-pace, but Monday to Saturday is different. You have quotas to fill. You see, it's a problem. How do you ask a man to shovel sand into a hole eight hours a day. Five and a half days a week. Plus unpaid overtime which is about two hours a day. Shovelling sand into a hole. Who wants that?"

"Do you fulfil your goals?"

"Yes."

"Always?"

"Yes. In fact we surpass them these days."

"Is production in Cuba rising?"

"Investments are beginning to pay off. So far production has been up and down or lagged badly. Our lean years."

I said, "The general pattern since the revolution has been falling production and broken promises, yet the masses still avidly listen to Fidel, the young support him, and there have been no defections from among the top leaders of the revolution. Why is that?"

"Because the revolution has been so logical. Get rid of the old order, push, push, push the people's education, guard their health, look around for the right things to grow and manufacture, solve nothing by force and think big. Underdeveloped people think in tens and twenties. Fidel has taught us to think in millions. On this programme the grass must grow. If not today, tomorrow. The people themselves are planting it. They are not waiting for manna from any government. Increasingly it's like that in Cuba. Democratic. The work and will of the people. Here we plant manna."

I said, "Has falling production been due to ignorance, or collectivization and lack of individual incentive?"

"Collectivization and incentive has less to do with it than, say, the weather. Look at the figures. Take sugar. One year up, one year down — 1965 six million, 1966 four-and-a-half million, 1967 six million, 1968 five million. The collectivization and incentives haven't changed but the figures change because of drought and problems of organization. Or take nickel, which is our second largest export. Same up and down picture. The factories we have were owned by the Yankees so we have acute spare-part problems. When we could make or buy the spare parts, production went up. When we couldn't, production went down. 1964 twenty-four thousand tons, 1965 twenty-nine thousand, 1966 nearly twenty-eight thousand, 1967 thirty-five thousand. In nickel like in everything else the Yanks have done everything in their power to sabotage us."

"How reliable are your production statistics?"

"You mean here or in Cuba generally?"

"Here."

"Well the work here is based on emulation between groups, group-rivalry, so everybody knows production statistics."

"What about national statistics, like the ten million tons?"

"Well, in sugar any small cane farmer can tell whether the claims made in his area are realistic. He can look at a cane-field, the conditions, the organization and make a fair assessment. It would be impossible for Castro to invent the ten-million-ton harvest and retain credibility here in Cuba. Another indication of credibility, of course, is the growing number of European capitalists who are extending credit to Cuba. And the growing Soviet credits."

I said, "Actually my fear about the ten million tons is not that the figure will be cooked, but that it will be achieved, if at all, by a state of excitement that can't possibly be kept up year after year on all fronts. I fear in the long run it's bad for business."

"Yes of course, of course," he answered, "but this generation needs Fidel's inspiration and the next generation will have technology and good work habits. Also what produces inspiration is not only Fidel's speeches, but his results. Getting ten million in 1970 will give us more confidence to do the same in 1971. We'll be more certain that organization works.

"In my experience organization is the best incentive. An ounce of organization is worth a ton of punishment. You see, I've organized this place so that the machinery doesn't break down and the supplies come in regularly so there are no hold-ups. That is something relatively new in Cuban factories, where things are always going wrong and workers enjoy the chance to hang about. For many years the revolution was one big breakdown in most of these places because we couldn't get spare parts — the blockade, the long journey from the Soviet Union, the lack of standardization — so we idled and joked half the week and the other half put in tremendous stints. It was dramatic, but not specially productive. The average was low, and some of the work was shoddy — the sort that comes from over-work. When there is widespread ignorance and things are disorganized people naturally can't function and mistakes have a chain reaction. Some of the workers look round for somebody to blame. Some drink rum and wait for the next disaster. And *Time* magazine, of course, called it all sabotage — which was at least flattering.

"You see, any agricultural project is an accumulation of scores of mechanized, skilled operations and we are still a highly unskilled people. We are still superstitious people who believe in magic and mystery and can never quite believe that one and one make two, every day, all the time. We wouldn't do the same thing two days running because we'd never believed it would work two days running — whatever power controlled things wasn't scientific. So all sorts of funny things happened. You mentioned the comrade who we sent up to Canada to buy a bull and he came back with a steer. Well, that steer probably ended up being artificially inseminated.

"And none of this is due to a lack of material incentive. With their free press and all, Yankees still seem very ignorant about basic things like politics. They can't last, can they? No, material incentives aren't important. The kind of thing that would have ruined Cuba would have been big wrong decisions like going ahead with industry ten years ago. Instead, Fidel switched back to sugar, where we at any rate had some know-how, and we earned the money and time to train engineers, who can now make a success of industry. But you've got to be organized. The ten million tons represents the kind of organizational effort that any advanced country would be proud of. It makes us agriculturally a developed country."

This man gave me the address of his daughter, whom I met with a group of political science students, sitting on the steps of the University of Havana.

I came in on the end of a gossip about a North American girl, a "peace-corp type", who had come down to have an affair with a party leader but the man got sick. She was short of money so she visited him in broad daylight in open hospital, and the indiscretion nearly killed him.

I introduced myself and they took me in their stride. The black girl in the group, the soldier/manager's daughter, started sending up Yankee sociologists who thought Cuba good for an article or a Ph.d. thesis.

"This revolution produces people who eat and wear clothes — you know, ordinary people. But eating is a marvel in Latin America, so the Yankees come down and study us and find bipeds, you know, ordinary bipeds with mouths, and they go away very excited about this zoo where the animals walk on two legs, and they put a knot in their handkerchiefs not to bomb us. One lady Yankee sociologist came down here, she was very sympathetic, she said how the only thing sociologists could predict was change, like the seasons, and how rebels became respectable, and how Havana University used to be a centre of protest and now it was a centre of the establishment — in other words, Cuban students should always protest, whether against Castro or Batista. I find it a little difficult talking to Yankees, especially sociologists, because they seem to me subnormal. I mean mentally deficient. They balance our new élite against our old élite, our economic failures against our economic success. That leaves a kind of blank in Cuba that I suppose makes them comfortable."

There was this black girl, her white boyfriend, a white girl and her black boyfriend. The black girl went on: "They think, Communism! Executions! Dead leaders! Even now, in 1970, they think that. Like they thought Fidel had killed Che. Imagine that! But the world is beginning to think — Capitalism! Napalm! Horrors! It's funny how they refer to Giron as their grave mistake, their disaster, ill-advised; never as barbaric and criminal. They don't think Giron! Kennedy! Mafia! They see themselves as civilized people ill-advised. Can you imagine reading in *Newsweek* or *Life* anything sensible?"

"Like what?"

"Not 'ill-advised' but 'criminal' and 'indictable'. You'd never get them to say that. They'd murder us first. They keep on seeing Cuban politics in exotic terms, charisma, Fidel's charisma, the ignorant Cuban people, a backward people, worshipping Fidel. They themselves of course, are rational and advanced. You know soon, not many years from now, they will wake up to the fact that the zoo on their doorstep is ordinary scientific twentieth-century Cuba. Like they woke up to Sputnik. They ... "

Her white boyfriend was listening, but the other couple were off on their own thing, and the black boy was saying petulantly: "I have no will-power. If I am sleepy I sleep. If I don't feel like, then I don't feel like. It is the only luxury I have, to indulge myself."

WHITE BOY: What's this?

WHITE GIRL: Nothing ... You were saying, Martha?

BLACK BOY: I'll tell you one thing. Compulsory military service is a pain in the arse. I wish I was a Yankee sociologist.

WHITE GIRL: You'd be in Vietnam.

BLACK BOY: Yes, the Yankees only train you for six weeks. Call you up, put a gun in your hand and advise you to wait till you see the flat of their nose. I like that ... Why is Cuba so full of petit-bourgeois black men with flat noses? Shoot them.

WHITE GIRL: I'm going home.

BLACK BOY: So long.

WHITE GIRL: Stop showing off.

BLACK BOY: Are you a Yank?

B.R.: No.

BLACK BOY: How do they feel, being the most criminal people in history?

BLACK GIRL: How do those Yanks see themselves?

B.R.: They feel they're a friendly neighbourly people who earn their money and pay their way.

BLACK GIRL: How do they feel about the Indians they killed?

B.R.: They believe the land belongs to those who use it.

BLACK GIRL: So if they use their own land it belongs to them. And if they use other people's land it belongs to them. In this sense they have a right in Latin America.

B.R.: Yes. They believe any development in Latin America is due to them, and perhaps to the Spaniards before them.

BLACK GIRL: I see. And they all believe this? The demonstrators don't believe it.

B.R.: The demonstrators are thought of as a noisy minority. The silent majority don't believe in demonstrating.

BLACK BOY: But they say that demonstrators show how free they are.

B.R.: Sometimes, yes.

BLACK BOY: So you have two systems — one where everybody eats, has a job, no fear of unemployment, a shabby but free place to live, free medical treatment for all, free schools for all, safe streets, no racism, reasonable equality. And another where some eat well, where there is unemployment and chronic fear of unemployment, a shabby expensive place to live, expensive medical treatment, very poor education for millions, crime in the streets, racism, inequality. Yet the first is worse than the second. Why? Because there are no elections. And what is the purpose of elections? To make sure that everybody eats, has a job, no fear of unemployment, a free place to live, free medical treatment and schools, safe streets, no racism, reasonable equality ... How do they pull it off? A sucker is born every minute, no?

They all laughed. He went on.

They seem to say that communism anywhere in the world threatens them. So they have troops everywhere, all over the world. Communism which has troops nowhere threatens democracy which has troops everywhere. They turn reason into a dirty joke. And the world's always like this. Why should one bother to live?

Then he suddenly turned all this into an attack on his girlfriend —

People lie with every glance, every shrug, every half-truth.

WHITE GIRL: People?

BLACK BOY: *You* run down some of your friends to please other friends.

WHITE GIRL: Don't be a fool. If I run people down they aren't friends.

BLACK BOY: To be precise, you say X's note to you is unimportant. You are slightly dismissive to me about it. And to him you're slightly dismissive about me. I don't want that.

He left. His girlfriend said nothing. The black girl was shocked at his suddenly equating grave public issues with personal ones. She said: "All these boring dots and commas that boy goes in for."

I said, "Isn't the revolution as much concerned with emotional pain as physical pain?"

"Yes, so let him try to find the causes of his pain so he can help other people, rather than moaning on about what she does with his little love notes."

"All right," said the girlfriend, "but let's not talk about it."

They all went on asking me questions.

QUESTION: What do Yankee students think of communism?

B.R.: Subconsciously the majority associate it with death and jail.

Q.: So we'll have to fight them?

B.R.: There's a very vocal minority who see communism as just another political system with rights and wrongs.

Q.: How do most people see the Vietnam war?

B.R.: They think armed communists from the North attacked South Vietnam and they came to the defence of South Vietnam.

Q.: But don't they know they are supporting Batista-type landlords?

B.R.: Yes, and they'd like to replace them with more liberal people.

Q.: More liberal landlords?

B.R.: Yes.

Q.: Do they know that according to Eisenhower eighty per cent of the Vietnamese people would have voted for Ho in an election?

B.R.: Yes, but they don't really believe a vote for communism can be a free vote. Something must be wrong somewhere and they want to put it right.

Q.: So on the strength of these beliefs they napalm and machine-gun dog, man, woman, and child.

B.R.: They believe their atrocities are far less than those of the Vietcong.

Q.: Do ordinary people know the facts about Vietnam? Why there's a brutal civil war?

B.R.: They just know it's a fight against communism and they support it.

Q.: What is the domino theory?

B.R.: The feeling that a communist victory in any part of the world ultimately threatens the United States.

Q.: But they have the H-bomb.

B.R.: Yes, but that doesn't secure them economically. Their trade and raw materials need to be secure.

Q.: So people fighting against US economic exploitation are a threat to the US?

B.R.: They support gradual change.

Q.: Why not immediate change, like in Cuba?

B.R.: I suppose they're waiting to see how things work out here, but immediate change wouldn't really suit their book. It might threaten their standard of living. Though many of them would deny this.

Q.: Their chief weapon for gradual change in Latin America is birth-control, isn't it?

B.R.: Yes.

Q.: But that isn't working. There are three hundred million Latin Americans now. There'll be six hundred million by the end of the century. And even if birth-control worked and Latin America could gradually become another United States — do we want another United States?

B.R.: Communism might mean Stalinism.

Q.: But it might not. And now capitalism means landlords and white terror.

B.R.: Anyway, as I said, a communist Latin America might be a serious threat to capitalism.

BLACK GIRL: Well it's up to Latin America to look after its own destiny. If those Yankee pigs know their own babies will die, and not only my babies, then they'll think twice. That is why we asked the Russians for rockets. So *their* beautiful white babies will burn. We want one, two, three Vietnams inside the United States of America.

In the book-shop next door to the University a retired high-school teacher told me, "There is serious mental starvation in Cuba — just about two books *per capita*, and mostly school books. These kids can't imagine a real bookshop, thousands of books, right-wing, left-wing books — cramming out the shops. And they don't understand the living faith of capitalism, the belief in *individual* efforts and initiative that those people live by. They don't know the enemy they are fighting. All they know about capitalism is Vietnam and black America. They don't know the real America, the thrift, the work, those beautiful white houses. They don't know too much about the tried and tested need for individual reward and incentive. Selfish yes, but that is what civilization is — the emergence of the individual from the herd."

I left, pondering on President Nixon as an emerged individual, then started thinking about those other emerged individuals in anti-communist Jamaica ninety miles away. In my Jamaican childhood the only place in Latin America I knew about was Quito, Ecuador, where there was a radio station broadcasting Yankee evangelism. For me this was Latin America, although my father, like a lot of Jamaicans, had gone to Costa Rica and Cuba in the twenties to find work. In Costa Rica he worked with United Fruit (I think as a time-keeper). One night a man chopped him several times with a machete. He was taken to hospital where they dipped his whole body in hot water to sterilize his wounds.

Once an Indian came to the hospital for attention, and they told him the doctor wouldn't be there till late so he waited outside all day. When the doctor arrived to attend him, he took off a cloth covering his belly and his guts fell out. That was life in our part of the world.

A Jamaican lady I met recently in London said how things were looking up in Jamaica now. The hundreds of thousands of unemployed and underemployed didn't want to work. The slums were there because people left their homes in the country for the bright city lights. The same would happen in Cuba if people were free to leave the countryside. She wasn't very interested in Cuba because everybody knew equality wasn't possible.

Like me, she had travelled fairly widely in North America and Europe but not in Latin America or Africa. She said she had little national consciousness. This didn't surprise me. Only the most urbane, cosmopolitan people could allow foreigners to ship away so much of their wealth.

In Jamaica we used to learn, we still learn, the geography of master-race countries — North America and Great Britain — and rattle off "Great Bear Lake, Great Slave Lake, Lake Athabaska and Lake Winnipeg", when we aren't rattling off "the spruce, the fir, the elder, the pine and the cedar". In my schooldays "A" wasn't for ackee, a vegetable which grew in the backyard, but for apple which was imported in December and stood on the King Street stalls, a splendid imperial red that became part of our colonial Christmas. Apples reminded us deliciously of desirable countries; so did the snow which we bought in the shops to decorate our Christmas trees made of pine. My mother couldn't afford pine so we made do with lignum vitae, which was merely local. But hanging from it were Christmas cards with white angels. Thirty years ago the nationalist movement introduced a few black angels, but they still haven't caught on. I remember those apples cost a shilling and had to be divided into four. They were hard and the most unforgettable luxury of all time apart from Libby's tinned pears.

These are the stock-in-trade memories of every colonial. They are minor symptoms of our inferiority, and like inferiors we rebel against these symptoms rather than against the root disease: economic dependence. Nowadays we feel liberated because "A" stands for ackee, and they are canned in a few two-by-four factories owned chiefly by North Americans, or local whites using cheap labour.

The existence of a few factories where before there were none means a steep rise in GNP and a black-faced government declares the country independent, democratic and gradually moving towards bread with liberty. A local army and police force deal with the mushrooming unemployed, most of them too young to vote. The eventual cure is apparently for them not to be born, and in the meantime, in nearby Puerto Rico, North American marines stand by to prevent another Cuba, where, according to a *Daily Gleaner* columnist, the government drains the blood of thousands of political prisoners before it shoots them, and sends it to aid the Vietcong.

More rational accounts of Cuba, by José Yglesias for example, are reprinted from the *New York Times*, but generally speaking in Jamaica communism means godless dictatorship and murder. The word carries with it nameless fears. The Jamaican road to development is to preserve law and order so as to encourage foreign investment, and to preach birth-control — which, however, is widely resisted as Nixon's plan to wipe out black people. The belief is that they castrate the men and reward them with a transistor radio which has one station, the Voice of America. Although in Jamaica *Granma*, along with Malcolm X, is banned, a few people are beginning to quote Castro who says that Cuba, once considered overpopulated, is now desperately short of people to develop the country; that in Europe the density is sixty per square mile, in Latin America only fifteen, that even in highly populated Europe blacks from various places are needed to do the dirty work.

The birth-control question is fairly academic, of course, since at best it takes three or four generations to have any noticeable effect and the Latin American masses mightn't wait, unless they are forced to by counter-revolutionary terror. It is this terror that the Cuban revolutionaries I met see as typically North American. Terror in the ghettoes, in the street, in Vietnam, in Latin America. Cubans no longer say, as they used to some years ago, that bourgeois liberty is a luxury underdeveloped people can't afford. They now take the view that bourgeois liberty is underdeveloped, that it boils down to freedom to exploit large sections of the world and the US population, and that everything else about it is a sham. Genuine democracy means mass political awareness; mass education and health; a humane concern for the next man, embodied in the ration book. To them capitalism doesn't have a leg to stand on because, taking even the lowest economic factor, a full belly, millions go hungry and undernourished in the United States. Communism is the quickest way for everybody to eat and live longer and vote in any way that matters. Terror is a bourgeois hangover and no essential part of communism, as Cuba has proven.

Castro promised bread without terror and so far has achieved it, but Cuba is a small country with a lot of Russian aid under its belt. Could the same freedom be achieved in a large, less aided Latin American revolution? Less Russian aid might be counterbalanced by use of Cuban experience, which could mean less costly mistakes, and given a cold choice the Latin American masses might even prefer the possible terrors of communism to the certain terrors of underdevelopment.

Castro said, on January 2, 1967: "Certain statistics provide a very eloquent description of what a revolution can mean to the life of a country. For example, let's take the yearly mortality rate per thousand inhabitants. In our country thirteen per thousand inhabitants used to die every year. This is the figure given by the United Nations. But now this figure has gone down to six-point-eight deaths per thousand inhabitants. This means that as a consequence of the revolution and the change in the people's living conditions, more lives are saved each year than were lost in the whole long period of revolutionary struggle. But this is not all. This figure is already the lowest in all of Latin America, and moreover, to our understanding, lower than that of Canada, which you all know is a considerably developed country."

This freedom from death and doctors' bills is as precious as any other liberty, and to get it, a widow told me, "you need not a vote but a gun. I am a widow," she said, holding my shoulder as she spoke, "and why? If we had these schools for doctors, these hospitals, I wouldn't be a widow. My husband get sick, my God, no place at the hospital, the doctor come here, glance round the room before he glance at my husband. I thought he was nosy about us living poor, but my mother said he was calculating if I could pay. Half his mind was on the money. So when Fidel talk about those days — terrible days when doctors were businessmen calculating their fees, I say shit on capitalism. How could I have trust in that businessman, so I call in another one. My God, those days. I tell you something, I caught myself worrying about the bill as much as José's health, just like the doctor, and I was ashamed. That money worried me. I ask God to forgive me. Before the second doctor came my husband died. José couldn't catch his breath and screamed for long hours. The son-of-a-bitch doctor came with golfsticks in his car, after José was dead. These children were babies and they don't remember, but there is a memory in Cuba and they are revolutionaries. Because of Fidel nobody dies screaming in their marriage bed. There are places for such things. If José was here I would be happy. The only thing I didn't like about him was that he beat the babies. José beating the babies used to make me sick and I thought about it when he was screaming to death. That and the money. God forgive me for it. That is another big change in Cuba. On this block people scarcely beat their wives and children. Christ, the beatings I used to get. My father caught me with my hand down here and cut me with rope. If he did that today he'd be in the people's court. No, I'll die for Fidel, but I'm not happy. Revolution makes you content but only God makes you happy. And in Cuba God is dead. Even me, brought up in Saint Joseph and Mary, I no longer believe any of it. God forgive me."

"Yes, I have a girlfriend," said one of the last men I talked to on the block. "Sometimes she comes here, or if my wife is here we meet outside. Nobody can tell me I must go to agriculture on Sunday. They encourage me to go sometimes, pull my leg, but I seldom go because I don't see enough of my wife and kids. I like what Fidel is doing for the country. Through Fidel I got an education. My wife wouldn't be a nurse if it wasn't for Fidel.

"We go to the pictures, eat out at restaurants, take the bus and go to the beach. We're out nearly every night, and the nights we stay in we watch television. We have a big family and we're always in and out. I wouldn't want to go to the United States, no, though at one time I wanted to do nothing else. They are interfering people. They meddle with what is not theirs. Cold-war people. They think their world is rich, and the system that creates that is freedom. This system must spread, and while the good grass grows the poor ass like me must starve. Well because of Fidel all that is dead now. Yes brother, Cuba is the first free territory in America."

Equality

The Cuban revolutionaries I met had at least two important things to say about equality. Firstly, they believe it is the driving force behind Cuban productivity, just as inequality — the fear of being among those left behind — is the driving force behind bourgeois productivity. Secondly, they take for granted a widespread consumer equality controlled by the ration book and are racing on to what they consider the only sound foundation for lasting equality — work-sharing, and the rise of the worker-intellectual.

In mass education the immediate question is whether everybody can be educated, and Cubans agree that some people have more natural intelligence than others, but see no reason for further rewards and punishments. In any case they feel that there is a tendency in bourgeois society to rationalize class differences and the division of labour by genetic theories. They believe sharing labour will mean decreasing the boredom and resentment of the masses and increasing their confidence. This in turn will affect their children's early environment — the most crucial factor for creating intelligence.

The environmental lag at present means that in spite of having the most ambitious educational programme in Latin America, with 27·6 of the population being educated (against a Latin American average of 16·8) nearly half of the two-and-a-half million children of school age still either don't attend school, drop out or fall behind. 400,000 don't attend, 138,000 drop out, 700,000 have fallen behind. Most of these children come from the poorest homes where there is no tradition of going to school. This lack of any mass tradition of education also accounts for the serious failure in the recruitment of teachers, compared with, say, doctors or agricultural technicians. The money they earn is roughly the same, so it isn't a question of incentives but of tradition. Doctors have an old glamour, agriculturalists a new one, but teachers are still merely school teachers. The revolution has to solve these obvious problems before it starts worrying about genetic inferiority.

The fear that people won't work or study unless individually rewarded is regarded as disproved by the success of the revolution. Cubans constantly underlined to me the fact that the day of individual research is dead, and pointed to the inventiveness shown by revolutionary teams — for example in the invention of spare parts that can't be obtained because of the US blockade. This Cuban drama of invention, of collectively finding ways round problems, now centres round the need to invent a machine to cut cane.

Attempts to build a cane harvester in other parts of the world have been unsuccessful, and the job was attempted by Soviet engineers who also failed.

Fidel announced a Cuban triumph on April 9, 1968.

"The workers and technicians of our machine industry, bent on finding a solution to the difficult problem of the mechanization of cane-cutting — which is one of the hardest, most arduous, most difficult jobs, one in which a man's productivity is insignificant, which requires hundreds of thousands of workers year after year to cut more than thirty million *arrobas* of sugar-cane per day by hand, during long months, one machete blow after another — took upon their shoulders an effort started several years ago: to build a cane-harvesting machine that would solve the problem once and for all. Two of these new combines were field-tested only a few days ago, and they were tested not with medium-yield cane, but rather with high-yield cane; not with easy-to-cut, erect cane, but with heavily strawed, tangled, reclining cane.

"And these machines — which are to undergo several improvements — performed astonishingly well: they picked up the tangled reclining cane, cut it, removed the straw, and deposited the cane stalks into the wagon, sufficiently clean to be directly processed at the mill.

"It is possible that no single thing will have a greater effect on the future of this country than these machines; it is possible that our people and future generations will owe few debts of gratitude as great as they owe to the men who designed and built these machines. They will mean the liberation of hundreds of thousands of workers from the most back-breaking work; they will multiply our workers' productivity many times over because . . . we aspire to have a considerable number of these machines by the year 1970 . . . We can affirm with full confidence that the present pace of our development will permit our agriculture to rank among the most advanced in the world."

The news was naturally epoch-making. The new combine operated by two men could cut between 25,000 and 30,000 *arrobas* a day, two hundred times as much as the most expert cane-cutter. (As one engineer said to me, "petrol is the best incentive".) If these machines could be produced and used on a mass scale it would substantially advance equality by cutting out the most enslaving work in Cuba. Unfortunately the announcement was premature — the sort of "loud-mouth optimism" that leads Fidel's enemies to abuse, detest and hopelessly underrate him, and re-inforces the opinion in the US that businessmen with incentives are needed to run a country.

Fidel casually mentioned the failure on July 14, 1969, consummately placing it in perspective.

"The revolution brought to our country the conditions for and the possibilities of mechanizing all work. But in the past workers had to struggle against machinery which displaced them. Dock workers had to struggle against bulk-sugar shipping, while now the problem is that, with the amount of merchandise and machinery being unloaded in our ports, we do not have enough dock workers. Today nobody will fight the installation of a bulk-sugar storehouse. On the contrary, everybody is happy to see it used. Why? Because there already exists an identification between the interests of the people and the means of production; now the means of production are not alien to the workers; now they are not used for the benefit of a privileged minority in detriment to the worker. Today machinery is the great ally of the worker.

"However, since the need didn't exist, due to problems I have explained regarding excessive labour force caused by under-development, cane-cutting combines were not developed. This is why, since the triumph of the revolution, we have been faced with the problem of finding a machine that would be effective in cutting cane, which, as you know, is a difficult plant — a plant unlike corn or rice which grows straight. No. Cane lies down, especially if it is of high yield. When it begins to surpass 750 hundredweight per acre it begins to bend with the slightest breeze; it becomes entangled and full of dead leaves clinging to the stalk. Building a machine that would lift, cut and clean the cane was a very difficult job.

"We have been working towards this goal for the last few years and, we have finally come up with a pretty efficient machine — the Libertadora. But the Libertadora is a complex machine which needs to be perfected. In this problem of mechanization it makes no sense to build thousands of machines that can't work when it rains or that are constantly having mechanical difficulties.

"Together with the Libertadora a simpler machine was built — the Henderson — which has a simpler system . . . It cuts the cane without stripping it of dead leaves and works in co-ordination with the cane-conditioning centres. A total of two hundred are being built. We plan to test them thoroughly, although results have been good up till now — so good that some days they have cut up to 5,000 hundredweight [fifty times as much as an ace cane-cutter]. For the moment this seems to be the best method, while the other combine is being developed."

After further successful trials the Government decided to try to build 1,000 Hendersons per year in 1971.

It may be that hopes of the Libertadora are fading, or that while it is being developed Fidel can't bear to cut by hand and is gambling a lot of money on Hendersons and cane-conditioning centres which will simply be scrapped if the Libertadora is perfected. This might not be excessively wasteful. The Hendersons are basically bull-dozers, which are always useful. But a private capitalist or a bureaucrat would probably find this kind of expenditure unforgiveable. Bureaucratic decisions made in an office are often going to be different from those made by workers in the field. Those who don't cut cane want to save money. Those who cut cane want to save labour. There is frequently a difference of interest between worker and bureaucrat and in fact some Cubans already feel that Cuban equality is being threatened by the rise of a new class of bureaucrats.

"The day after Fidel clamped down on the *dolce vita*, V took her own children to school for I think two mornings, then on the third day her nanny rose again. When I see her picture in *Granma*, all dark-glasses like a Yankee tourist, meeting foreign ladies and dining them in traditional Cuban high style, I wonder where's the guerrilla? If I say this, of course everybody jumps down my throat saying V is pushing forty-five and has to climb Turquino peak to get the children to school, but what about those who have to climb Turquino peak and don't have nannies? Fidel tells all the comrades to work like hell for nothing while he works like hell for steak — huge steaks. And so on down the line. My ex-husband, who lives just over the way, is a bureaucrat and of course we lived the life — nice house, two cars. Yes, he still has two cars in the garage there right now, and he just had a new cyclon fence put up. You can go and look at it. And he'll have a bottle of rum. Not any old rum, the best rum. It's funny, but my husband could always tell his 'workers' to put the revolution first, and it never occurred to them to tell him where to get off. They were probably so astonished that the bosses worked at all that they expected them to eat more. Yes, there's definitely a new class in Cuba — you just listen to my husband talk — *his* workers, *his* men. This is what they are teaching the students at the university — 'Go into the farms and factories and find ways to make the people work and study and get cultured.' There are two classes in Cuba — those uncultured people who work, and those cultured people who find ways to make them. So little notes come regularly from party headquarters to managers, saying you can't appeal to workers if you're corrupt and parasitic. But the poor managers never think it applies to them because after all they *have* to be at meetings, it's their job, and they *have* to use their cars to get to them, and the cars have chauffeurs and the meetings go on all day so they need food, and which Cuban is going to turn down lunch and dinner and cigars? That's like showing a bed to a whore and expecting her to be at a loss. And anyway who are the people sending them these notes? Men who flick away the cigar ash as they dictate. Really the secretaries must laugh. I am one, I laugh. Of course this corruption is enough to cripple any country but fortunately there are these large numbers of workers, obedient little slaves who admire high-living managers and feel full-bellied watching the boss eat. Now all this rubbish sets up a lot of hatred in work places, because you have sensible workers surrounded by all these house-slaves, and wanting to retch. But really they have no case, because Cuba is not calling for justice but for production, which is another matter. And there are enough Cubans who worship brute force and organized power to win the production battle. They'll produce mountains of food then trot off to prove their *machismo* in one, two, three Latin American Vietnams."

I tried to talk to this woman's ex-husband, who was the twenty-eight-year-old manager of a very large plant. I walked into his house, he couldn't see me — was just rushing off. I telephoned his office, he couldn't see me — too busy, going on a journey. Finally I made it, walked into his office and heard a worker demanding wages for days he didn't work.

How could he work, he said. There were no guards on the machine and it was illegal to use it without guards, so he wasn't at work. He'd asked time and again for a safe machine and didn't get one, so no work. But he wanted his wages for the days he couldn't work since it wasn't his fault. He turned from the manager to the personnel manager who was trying to calm him —"Aren't they to pay me?"

"Yes, yes, we just want to talk."

The door closed, and any hope of an interview.

Several days later, after making an appointment, I caught the manager, again on his way out, and squeezed in a few words about the quarrel.

"No, there was no guard on the machine, so why didn't the comrade fit one? There are rods outside; that's all it needs. He says I never told him that. Any man I have to tell that isn't alive. I don't want any zombies round here."

"I notice he's on another machine."

"Yes, the comrades could see my point. They got fed up with him and pushed him off onto this old machine. So he's lost his new machine and his wages."

"But you've lost him, haven't you?"

"The workers ended up against him. It's through using difficulties like these that you run a plant. Maintain discipline. The personnel manager wanted me to call him up before some elaborate meeting. Fink."

A Young Communist in this factory smiled about the manager's perks.

"People eat when the food's there. They don't feel guilty because they can take it or leave it. Fidel left a life full of food to go hungry in the Sierra."

His friend, one of the new Cuban breed of worker-intellectuals, a Young Communist who spoke Russian, heard this, came over and said: "I am one of those people against all privileges, including Fidel's. It is very easy to say we're not yet in communism and make exceptions. You make an exception of Fidel, and then of yourself. The correct attitude to Fidel's privileges," he laughed, "is the attitude of the revolution — that bourgeois people who were used to a house and servant and enormous meals, like Fidel, can go on having them because they are used to them. These are what we call historical privileges, meaning history accounts for them, and they are understandable. Our laws provide for that. There are bourgeois now drawing pensions and still in their big house so they live as they used to live — completely idle. But unless we understand that these are historical privileges we will start imitating them — like this guy in the office who must stop using factory transport as private property, and stop kicking people around."

What did this young man think of the incident with the worker and the unsafe machine?

"Very serious."

"Why?"

"Because the worker hates the power situation in the factory and wanted an excuse to revolt. The manager uses power all the time; enjoys beating people down. That's authoritarianism. The Young Communists will call a meeting."

"Fidel hired the manager. Who fires him?"

"The Ministry hired him. The workers will fire him."

"But not if he gets excellent results?"

"If the Young Communists are discontented, then how is that an excellent result? That is a very serious result. We'll have to go into the incident and draw correct conclusions, that's all. It was high-handed. No, he'll change his ways or leave. For example, we've reminded him once again that he must do his stint on the factory floor, and he's agreed."

"But he's agreed before."

"Yes, and now we've reminded him."

"Why do the workers like him?"

"He's a good manager. The quotas get overfilled. But in the long run this kind of good management is not going to work, because workers who put up with high-handed bureaucrats are under-developed. A neo-colonialist mentality is possible even in socialism. This manager, for example, encourages production at the expense of study. Everybody knows studying is hard. Most of the young people in this factory would rather work. They have to be coaxed to study, and end up going through the motions. People can very soon get psychologically divided into upper-class students and lower-class labourers — with all the emotional rage and guilt that goes with it." He said he had read recently that the psychological rot started in school where they value, not the knowledge, but the kudos of high marks.

"High marks, low marks. Queens and drones. That is class education. At present only about fifteen to twenty per cent even of party members are studying. The Young Communists will increase the percentage in this plant, particularly among young workers. With proper care *everybody* will be educated, *every man* with his own talent, and we must work for that. Now. Not when the production battle is over. This manager feels that if people have brains they will study and get high marks, and the duds will be labourers. At the meeting we'll sort all this out."

We sat on a box eating an adequate lunch. His friend had gone to some other part of the factory to beat up support for the meeting. This factory was huge and make-shift, but fairly clean. The lavatory seat wasn't falling off. There was grease on the wash-basin, and no soap, but otherwise the place was clean. There were beautiful posters about "conscience" and "absenteeism" all round. Outside, a blackboard on the wall displayed chalked-up quotas. There was a cartoon on a notice board about an absentee legally changing his name (names of absentees are sometimes called out in assembly), and a notice about an inter-factory baseball game, which some keen young men were talking about. One was already making the winning shots, and the others shouted "*azucar*" and "*cana*" — sugar and cane: baseball shots are given these names; propaganda for the ten million tons successfully worked into sport. I mentioned to the Young Communist that they seemed to ignore the cartoon and he said it had been there for days. In any case, "some can hardly read", he laughed. He really seemed determined to wipe illiteracy off the face of the earth and on this subject he spoke with none of the famous communist politeness and restraint.

"This fool [the manager] actually uses the bourgeois phrase 'equal opportunity'. I'll tell you about equal opportunity. Before the revolution the woman in the house next door to our hovel used to look down on my mother for allowing me to run barefoot after Yankee tourists. She would come smiling into our shack to save my mother's soul and pray with her, glancing at my body because I didn't have a shirt on, I'll never forget that, and I was ashamed that my mother knelt down to pray. I remember thinking, 'she'll be sending me to school next'. I was ten, and I was saving up for a shoe-shine box that would become a chain. I saw the whole chain lined up, like smart shoes. I'd end up owning the town. When this woman and my mother stopped praying and started singing, I felt as if I didn't know my way any more; my mother, who used to be sensible like me, was backsliding into school and religion and I ran out of the house to find my own bearings. Didn't come back for weeks. That woman next door meant school and church and I kept my distance. I don't think I ever looked at her. So what's the use of saying that boys like me had equality of opportunity? And it's the same with the majority of young people in this factory who are thinking only about finding a girlfriend or husband. They go about absent-minded thinking 'Can I make her tonight? No, wait, put it off. Be patient in the attack.' That is the only guerrilla activity they are thinking about, capturing a girl, lying in ambush, just as all this manager thinks about is striding across the floor, and having men stop their work to notice him. This man is a monkey. Equality is foreign water to him. You say he kept you waiting. I've seen him invite a comrade into his office, keep him waiting a whole morning, then deal with him in five minutes. There is a law that machines must have proper guards on them. He can't get away with penalizing the worker. Bourgeois society reflects the injustice of men like him — prisons, mad-houses, incredible ghettoes, class systems and colour problems."

"If you're having a meeting about that incident, can I come?"

"I'll let you know."

A little black man who worked in the factory saw me in the street later on and cadged a cigarette. He was never absent from work, he said, because it was more bother to be absent than to work. Yes, the boss had a house. Some people had houses and some still didn't have. The newest houses went to the most needy. What sort of house did he himself live in? Very bad, because the country was behind in construction. Men couldn't be spared from the cane-fields. But it might be better next year if they got the ten million. If not, woe-betide. All work in the country would stop except cutting cane. With Fidel it was eggs or young ones. What did he think of the manager? Formidable. Not the sort of man you could hold in your mouth. Had he heard about the incident on the floor? Oh yes, an everyday thing. Cubans were very fiery. No, he wasn't aware that the Young Communists wanted an enquiry. They were formidable as well.

He's in a hurry, I want to talk, I follow him. He's in two minds about shaking me off. We get to a room in a block, packed with men, a bottle of rum passing round like communion wine. In the centre two cocks, necks flaring, one brown, one black, called Fidel and Raul. Their spurs were straight steel spears. Intense, electric support. No betting that I could see, only the bottle of rum passing. I sort myself out a little space. Shouts and hugs. First blood. Fidel breathes through his blood. No intention in the world of giving in, but after sparring and passing and drowning in blood he suddenly drops. His throat's torn out. Raul tries to get at his head. Fidel holds his head in, resting, perhaps feigning a little. A little panic creeps into Raul, trying to get at the head. He makes peevish futile thrusts. Fidel lunges, wounds. Both lie on the ground. Shouts of "Raul", "Fidel", "Raul", "Fidel". Fidel drags himself along and kills. Yes, there's money passing. And there's our manager, lapped in the marvellous illegal fraternity of a gambling hell. I catch his eye and he shows absolutely no embarrassment. He says, "hi," and goes on laughing. On the way out he says to me, "Some poor woman will have to wipe up this mess." I try to line up an interview for the next day. Very busy. The day after that — no again, very busy. The week following? OK, at his house.

We started talking in his drawing-room which had only a wooden table, a few chairs, and a clean floor. We ended at the office where he had to get some work done. There was rum, but it stayed in the cupboard. With certain Cubans, as with certain people everywhere, hospitality flows unless you're black, for example, or low-class, or otherwise unimportant. I said, "How do you see this business of perks?"

"Well they mustn't become a habit, because any time you might be out in the fields for six months, a year, two years."

"In the last four years how often have you been out in the field?"

"Four years ago I was out for the whole year. The next year for two months — I had this job. The next for six weeks. This year — God knows. I'm here till 2 a.m. many a morning. Most people here work shorter hours than me."

"But boring work, and not many perks."

"Work is work."

"And perks are the luck of the draw?"

"No, once you start having half an eye to a cushion for your backside you're a dead man."

"Why two cars?" He lit up a cigar to allow the impudent curiosity to float away outside.

"You think I go round collecting cars? They belong to this place and I keep an eye on them."

"And use them?"

"Of course. A man in my position shouldn't waste time. And why take the bus? It is uncomfortable. In Cuba we are levelling up, not down. If a car helps a man get results, give him a car. Results are the problem now. Equality is a future problem. We will think about that tomorrow."

"Why the new fence?"

"I saw it somewhere and liked it, and it was offered me."

"Doesn't that kind of thing give offence?"

"To my ex-wife, yes. The workers reckon I have a fence because I do my job. One problem at a time. The problem now is to get people to work without coercion. If we have really solved that problem, think what it means for Latin America."

"You think that in future all workers will share in management?"

"Various groups of workers run this factory right now — vanguard workers, Young Communists, the union, plus the administration. Certainly all those who are capable share in management. You can't ask people who aren't capable."

"And you think there will always be such incapable people?"

"That's an educational fact. All this elaborate equality is in the future. The battle now is to eat. In a place like this, all right, rotation of managers, yes, of course, but you need discipline. The boss needs touch — what do I mean, touch, touch, green fingers, whatever you plant grows. You know students come here, young political scientists, and they want to know why I don't have problems — well what can I tell them? I could say the answer is discipline. It's there in my eyes, the way I walk, my rhythm, the pitch of my voice. I tell them the answer is not in books. Take Che. Genius is a bolt from the blue. D'you know that in Cuba we've solved all the main problems that plague east and west. In agriculture we're farming on a scale that the Yankees and Europeans with their minifundia cannot match. And we don't have the incentive problems of the Soviet block because people here don't live and die for what they can buy in a shop. They become interested in solving problems, not consuming. Our economy has the simplicity of genius. Why? Because there are millions of men ready to go wherever we tell them. A hundred thousand go into the fields to cut cane. We will swim in goods. We will swim in leisure. Within fifteen years Cubans will be better fed, clothed, educated than the average Yank. And this is the result of organization — the chain of command."

"Can I come to that meeting about the worker you disciplined?"

He was surprised. "Of course. Certainly. It's a little meeting. It's nothing."

All the powers in the factory were represented at the meeting: the party, the Young Communists, the advanced workers, the union and the administration.

MANAGER: I am not a hundred per cent sure of the purpose of the meeting, so I insisted on an informal thing with a few comrades . . .

ADVANCED WORKER: The meeting is about the incident which everybody agreed was well handled and finished with. Who doesn't agree?

FIRST YOUNG COMMUNIST: (*Veiled sarcasm*) Well, comrades, shall we just vote and get back to work?

UNION: What is the problem?

SECOND YOUNG COMMUNIST: Any comrades who . . . The general problem . . .

The first Young Communist, the one who talked to me, cut in . . .

FIRST YOUNG COMMUNIST: There is one demand made on the comrades. High production . . .

ADVANCED WORKER: This meeting is taking up time. We should be producing.

FIRST YOUNG COMMUNIST: Well if all we're concerned with is production . . . There should be other demands besides high production.

PERSONNEL MANAGER: But how does this apply to the disciplined comrade? That's what we are here about.

MANAGER: We're right in the middle of a very difficult quota in the plant. We mean to achieve it. To surpass it (*applause*).

UNION: We had a little discipline problem. Why are we digging it up?

ADVANCED WORKER: I don't see why we are digging it up.

MANAGER: Let's get back to work.

ADVANCED WORKER: (*Rising*) Meeting-mania . . .

FIRST YOUNG COMMUNIST: The tactic is to use slogans about the job and filling quotas to stampede us out of here. I don't know if anybody really believes that *we* need reminding . . .

PERSONNEL MANAGER: We accept that, comrade.

MANAGER: What is the problem?

FIRST YOUNG COMMUNIST: We're still being stampeded. We think the comrade should have been encouraged to fit a guard. This would have improved management/worker relations because that comrade's view is that the revolutionaries are the new bosses and all he had to do is like it or lump it, and that is very serious. Work in a factory is not only for production. It is for integrating people into the revolution. For integrating Cubans into the Cuban revolution. The majority of people who work here are not vanguard workers or party members. They come here because they have to work. And if we write them off as unrevolutionary material — no, no, that is impossible. This comrade should have been advised to fit a guard, but now there is too much bad blood for that. It is too late.

PERSONNEL MANAGER: The comrade was advised by the manager to fit a guard.

FIRST YOUNG COMMUNIST: He says he wasn't.

MANAGER: He says, of course . . . Clearly . . . But what I want to underline to every comrade is that people become integrated into the revolution because they see the revolution means business (*applause*). The revolution delivers. No fooling about that.

ADVANCED WORKER: Before this manager came here we weren't delivering. These comrades know that.

MANAGER: And they know you can have a Sunday school that delivers nothing (*laughter*).

UNION: I move that as far as the disciplined comrade is concerned we let well alone and get on to the other problems.

MANAGER: What problems?

FIRST YOUNG COMMUNIST: None at all. A comrade has lost his machine, his wages, but no problem.

UNION: He can appeal to the jury.

FIRST YOUNG COMMUNIST: He won't bother.

SECOND YOUNG COMMUNIST: Why don't we pay the comrade, and advise him to fit a guard if he wants back his machine?

MANAGER: Not a cent.

ADVANCED WORKER: Why don't we lick his arse?

PERSONNEL MANAGER: There is such a thing as weakness.

MANAGER: Weakness would run like dry-rot through this place. And I was holding my tongue, because tongues run away with people, and discussion is easy, but let me answer the young comrades: discontented workers could never produce what we are producing in this factory. They could never achieve our attendance record, our overtime record.

FIRST YOUNG COMMUNIST: Too many people here do practically no overtime. They vote to do overtime and then don't do it. Our average is high because of the phenomenal production of the advanced comrades. Facts like this don't stop us winning a Moncada banner, but . . .

Mention of the banner was Pavlovian. The comrades salivated, and seemed for no other reason to be more attentive.

FIRST YOUNG COMMUNIST: Those who do no overtime are a discontented minority. Is this necessary? We don't want any helpless minorities in Cuba. The treatment of this man was scornful and tactless, and we called this meeting because this was not the first time . . .

ADVANCED WORKER: On the other hand we don't want any liberalism, comrades, no liberalism whatsoever.

UNION: It's a little matter that has blown over.

ADVANCED WORKER: I say close the case and get back to work. We have a good factory going, and as the comrade said we didn't get that by having meetings every twenty-four hours.

PARTY: I vote that we close the case.

FIRST YOUNG COMMUNIST: (*To advanced worker*) But you mustn't misquote Fidel.

ADVANCED WORKER: How?

FIRST YOUNG COMMUNIST: Fidel said "no liberalism whatsoever" in dealing with counter-revolutionaries. This man is not a counter-revolutionary. No Cuban who obeys the laws and works eight hours a day is a counter-revolutionary.

MANAGER: We all understand the concern, let's bear it in mind and wrap this up, go back to work and win the banner. Win the banner comrades, win the banner. This is the job.

(Applause. A comrade stands up to leave)

FIRST YOUNG COMMUNIST: With higher morale *all through the factory* we increase production. That act of indiscipline was a bad sign of low morale. What I suggest is that we ask for volunteers among the less revolutionary comrades to fit a guard on the machine and then give the comrade the option of going back to it when we've paid him his wages.

UNION: If this would raise morale . . .

SECOND YOUNG COMMUNIST: We must follow the policy of integrating everybody.

FIRST YOUNG COMMUNIST: We are chasing production and what is the scientific way to do this? By integrating everybody, and by educating everybody. We are not doing either of these things. We are not integrating, and not educating. If this factory neglects education there will be a short-term gain in production, but a long-term loss. That is no way to win the banner of the Heroes of Moncada.

ADVANCED WORKER: *(Salivating)* Hear, hear!

UNION: I am with that.

ADVANCED WORKER: Now I am with that. I am with education. That is a far more important matter.

FIRST YOUNG COMMUNIST: Workers are not studying for the following reasons: irregular attendance of teachers; inadequate facilities; overwork *(laughter)*. There is a lot of merely formal attendance at night school.

MANAGER: All this needs a full meeting. We can't discuss this here.

ADVANCED WORKER: But I am one hundred per cent with all this, and we must all see to this. We must provide the requisite facilities and the requisite persuasion, because we are one hundred per cent behind this.

MANAGER: Fidel himself, Fidel himself reminds us, comrades, about doing too many things at once, and ending up as bad workers and bad students.

PARTY: We must bear that in mind, by all means.

ADVANCED WORKER: We must be good workers and good students.

MANAGER: We must discuss all this at a full assembly, all workers, everybody, and see what we can come up with. It could even be a community undertaking. Anyway we will see.

FIRST YOUNG COMMUNIST: Not see comrade, make sure.

ADVANCED WORKER: We will make sure.

FIRST YOUNG COMMUNIST: With integration in mind, and legality, let's pay the comrade and ask him to fit a guard if he wants to work on that machine.

MANAGER: But then where is my authority?

ADVANCED WORKER: No liberalism whatsoever.

UNION: I vote we do something about the guard, give the comrade the option of going back, and forget about the wages.

PARTY: The wages aren't needed, anyway.

FIRST YOUNG COMMUNIST: That comrade has nine children, and only three of them have scholarships.

MANAGER: Three children with scholarships! Full board and lodging for three children, and the bastard can't fit a guard.

FIRST YOUNG COMMUNIST: Well let's pay him and ask him to fit the guard.

MANAGER: Not a cent.

PARTY: Let's repair the guard, because that's all it needs, leave it to the comrade to go back or not, and suggest that he appeal to the jury about the wages.

FIRST YOUNG COMMUNIST: Yes, agreed, and the manager would be the best person to inform him of all that.

MANAGER: Matters of personnel are to be dealt with by the personnel manager.

ADVANCED WORKER: I think we've found the best way out once again.

UNION: A very good meeting.

MANAGER: (*Suddenly full of baseball*) What's the score against Orientales?

I left the factory tailed by five ten or twelve-year-old black children, throwing questions at me. They asked what I liked about Cuba. I asked what they thought about Cuban equality. They said "Is Cuban equality famous?"

"Where?"

"Isn't Cuba famous all over the world?"

"Some people think that everybody is hungry without exception." They laugh. I point to a long queue and they all come back at me playfully, hitting at me with their books — "What would happen if the food was all shared where you come from? The queues would be that long" — they play around, making an endless queue. I say, "You tell me about Cuban equality."

"Everybody eats the same and wears the same clothes and studies the same books, goes to doctor, free baseball, free toys. What more?" They ran across the road to an ice-cream parlour and shouted at me, "gets the same ice-cream."

I catch the children's zaniness and make up rhymes as I walk:

Some are bright and some are dim,
And food's expensive;
So some must sink and some must swim
To preserve incentive ...

I go back towards the ice-cream parlour and shout to the children: "Why does Fidel eat more than your father?"

"Because he has a bigger appetite. Of course, naturally. He is a big fat man."

"Because," says another, "you need lots of meat to go on television and talk for so long. Talk, talk, talk ... " He makes his hands into a mouth and mimes filling it with food. Another says, "Because he is Prime Minister." The smallest one says that Fidel doesn't eat more than *her* father.

As luck would have it I see the worker who was disciplined, in the ice-cream parlour with five of his children. He didn't want to talk about the incident. The boss was the boss he said scornfully, like of old. Everybody had the same ration book, but not the same rations. I told him about the meeting. He was silent but gratified. I asked would he go back to his machine? If there was a guard, yes, he said.

And would he appeal about the wages? "Yes, yes." He suddenly tried to get the waitress to change his order. He was hungry, he said. Too many shortages.

I left depressed, suddenly fearing, for some reason, brutally sense-less war, two or three Vietnams. And what for? Why war? Why bomb and blockade Cuba?

"If it is a grave charge that Cubans don't vote, why isn't it equally grave that Yankee factories run under capacity in a hungry world?" The Young Communist had said that to me, and there is no answer.

"People need liberty certainly," he had said, "but chiefly after they have food. And in Cuba there is a strong tide towards both food and liberty." This seemed to me true, and to make Cuba the most important country in the Western world.

In Cuba the word *socio* means buddy and there is a well-known joke that sociolism reigns, not socialism. I asked a member of the Central Committee of the Communist Party where the manager of the factory I'd visited got his house. He said probably the same place he got his fence. It wasn't important, since the vast majority of houses were being built for workers on the state farms who had nowhere decent to live.

"For us equality is good economics as much as idealism. The minute we develop an élite in Cuba, voluntary labour is dead; and this country runs on voluntary labour: our greatest effort, the ten million tons, is based on voluntary labour and the sharing of dirty work. Clearly no man is going to cut cane if the Major is at the beach with his wife and a basketful of fried chicken."

"But what about cutting cane side by side with some major who arrives in a car and goes home to fried chicken?"

"The people don't worry about that much because they know on the whole the leaders have more responsibilities, and are working like hell for general abundance. And better yet, are achieving it. There is a broad equality which justifies voluntary labour; and voluntary labour is the central tool of this revolution. It was Che's creation, Che's weapon. It was tried, as you know, in Russia but its hour hadn't come and it gave way to individual incentives, but Che pushed it through in Cuba. Che believed that even if most people are selfish and suffering from 'human nature', some have idealism which should be harnessed. For example, you have a factory full of selfish people who won't even come to work, so instead of threatening them with unemployment you call on the few idealists in the factory to do the work, express their idealism in deeds, work ten, twelve, eighteen hours a day till the plan is fulfilled. What the loafers drop, the revolutionaries pick up. Idealism takes over as the force that runs the factory and this spreads, because logically if I go into a factory and work long hours so that the idler beside me can eat exactly the same rations, it makes him uneasy. Che's voluntary labour is the key to revolution without terror, and you can't have voluntary labour without equality."

"Some of the most crucial plans in Cuba are fulfilled by soldiers earning about eight pesos a month. How voluntary is that?"

"Well, there again you have the saving ten per cent. Enough of them are keen, so those guys fight to get into the Che Guevara trailblazers brigade which contains the most over-worked sonsabitches in Cuba."

"Does the brigade eat more than the rest of the population?"

"Yes, they need a big bellyfull for heavy work. But they could stay in camp and eat modestly and not work day and night all week. No, these are men rising to a challenge."

"Is promotion the incentive?"

"The general principle in Cuba is to promote very slowly, so ask any member of the brigade whether he's after promotion and his answer would be — 'No, not personal promotion, but I like to be well thought of in a famous brigade. I want to belong to a brigade that is worthy to bear Che's name. I want to be worthy to honour Che.' In Cuba we are no longer afraid that everything is tied up with money, so we can genuinely admire other men like Che because they are expressing genuine idealism.

"Any future Latin American revolution," he said, "must use voluntary labour as a central revolutionary principle. In the early years how would we have solved the unemployment problem without voluntary labour? You know what happened; at the revolution's triumph there was vast unemployment. Well, we sent some to school and used the rest building an infrastructure, paid for with the assets we seized from the Yanks, plus red gold later on. Also we padded the existing work-places a bit. So what happened? With full employment all the bare-foot people wanted easier jobs. The sugar-workers got out of the sun and into air-conditioned offices making coffee for bureaucrats. Nearly every Cuban who could, found himself a sinecure. Without voluntary labour to cut the cane we would have had to whip all those people back into the cane-fields. Instead the army of conscience swarmed over the fields, cutting cane. They ruined some of it but there was a net gain, because money gradually became a secondary matter in Cuba. It was no longer a silver scale with which men carefully weighed out their labour to the nearest ounce. Wage slavery was abolished, *chico*. That bull-shit is over. You know, voluntary labour nearly killed me. I couldn't face manual work. Say manual labour to a Cuban and he says yes, yes, all right, but really his back isn't shaped that way. Now every Cuban child picks coffee at ten and cuts or weeds cane at fifteen as part of education. Look, I am not absolutely certain of this but I think it's true: I've watched members of the Central Committee, none of whom are loafers, shake hands with members of the Che Guevara brigade, but not as equals. I almost think the brigadists were superior. It certainly happened to me. Labour is fashionable.

"So then voluntary labour makes full employment possible, and also full production — every factory and farm working to capacity. People can speed up without fear of putting themselves out of work. Technology becomes possible, indeed necessary. Education becomes necessary. Graduates are no longer begging in the street, like in Mexico. All that is miraculous in this part of the world. You see what is happening in the Soviet Union. A glut of college graduates fighting for professional work. It's no use telling them about the dignity of labour. What dignity is there in sweeping up after a football match? The only honest thing is to make every man combine skills with brute work, and make him learn this when he's young. That's the programme now in this country. They're in a real bag in the Soviet Union. As I understand it their system of bourgeois education is so good that they are not producing enough factory labour. They'll have to end up paying labourers such high wages that children will be tempted to give up studying. In the States they solve the problem by having one education for blacks, and one for whites. But really, those people are cynical. The military-industrial complex only cares about winning, beating the arse off communism, and they provide cynical rationalizations about freedom for those who need them."

I assured him this wasn't true. All nations believe passionately in their own myths, and go righteously to war. The myths are convenient and ensure they stay aggressively ahead, but still they believe in them. This of course made mere belief as worthless as mere cynicism.

"Oh well," he sighed, "let's not discuss them." He went on, "Now I've told you that equality is a mass incentive, but what about individual incentive? By and large one follows the crowd. But still people are individuals with a basic need for uniqueness. This is satisfied in bourgeois society by phoney individualism — making shoes in all colours and shapes. The 'really' individual girl wears her skirt shorter than anyone and the 'really' individual boy grows his hair longer. The 'original' artist stops doing what was done yesterday in his own country, and does what was done yesterday in other countries. Or else some charming eccentricity makes him an individual. In capitalism only a relatively few people can express genuine creativity, genuine individuality, because most work is uncreative — handing goods over a counter. And most people are fairly uneducated, without informed ideas. Here the way is opening. When the dirty work is shared all round, then everybody will have the time and the mind to be creative."

This idea of creativity through release from brute labour challenges the view that socialism results in dreary equality. Bourgeois democracy, with its assumption that genius is rare and lonely, and that the fittest survive aided by the scholarship system, is often unimpressed by any emphasis on the mass, the multitude, everybody. But perhaps this mass does end up having a decisive effect on bourgeois standards of culture and creativity. Bourgeois culture, for example, venerates the arts more than the sciences; the household names are not generally the scientists but the artists. Why? Because art is easier and cheaper than science and as a result literacy is more widespread than numeracy. Science needs tools which are too expensive, and an exactness too demanding, for free and easy I-know-what-I-like taste. It would be nice to think that art flourished because science on the whole is too basic — saves life, lengthens it or merely makes it more comfortable — whereas art raises more subsequent questions — what to do with the life that's saved. But really art is all we know. It is the product of our unaided senses and boils down to simple, if delightful, insights, rhythms, forms. Children sometimes produce it. Our cultural values are relatively undemanding, of the Sunday newspaper kind. One only has to look at our wage-scales, which often reflect our values. A young primary school teacher in London or New York gets less than a young typist, and if she can't live on it, why then, let her type. The prevailing values of the society are commercial, i.e. easy and undemanding, and culture doesn't escape this.

It is reasonable to suppose that a more complex culture would result from a more enlightened mass, not devoted to mindless brute labour.

The first stage in the development of voluntary labour in Cuba was to deal with the aversion of bourgeois culture to manual work so it could more easily be shared. Going into the fields became respectable. People didn't produce very much, but this was unimportant. In any case millions of individuals producing a little produce a lot. The second stage, now under way, is to deepen people's understanding of shared labour as the key to a classless, educated society and to raise individual productivity, express revolutionary idealism in work, break the economic bottlenecks that choke men with hunger and frustrate their ideals everywhere.

The great symbol of this second stage was the 1970 goal of a ten-million ton sugar harvest, described by Herbert Matthews of the *New York Times* as "certainly beyond the range of probability". The work was to be done largely by volunteers, they were to cut as much as they could, and among them there was no question of piece-work. The incentive was conscience, not money.

"The forces ready to be mobilized," said Castro, "are great. We think that by March there will be approximately 350,000 men in the countryside, 350,000 men. We must say that, due to a series of reasons, organization in some cases, faulty leadership in others, problems with the cane-loading machines and hauling, and even a lack of awareness on the part of many of our workers, of awareness of the importance of the sugar crop and the importance of work for our country in these years — the amount of cane cut daily has been low . . . In addition we must say that estimates for this harvest have been based on relatively low cane-cutting averages. We believe that 200,000 men in the countryside working eight hours — eight hours! — can cut all the cane needed for the ten-million-ton harvest. Of course, not everybody has the same productive capacity; not everybody has the same experience, the same skill. But the cane-cutters know what a man can cut in . . . eight hours — an average man. We're not talking about ace cane-cutters. A brigade in Oriente province from the Ministry of the Revolutionary Armed Forces averaged more than two hundred hundredweight per day per man in August . . . Considering the heat in that province in that month, we must say that those comrades are gifted with extraordinary physical endurance, with tremendous resistance to heat. Well, we're not talking about those cane-cutters. But it can be stated that really, in four hours an average cane-cutter can cut thirty hundredweight of cane, with some difficulty. Moreover an average cane-cutter can cut fifty hundredweight in eight hours. At the beginning some people cannot cut that much. They cannot cut it in the first ten or fifteen days. But at the end of the month they can cut it, average cane-cutters can. Of course it is necessary that they go to the countryside with the idea of cutting cane. There are some cane-cutters who in our opinion work harder cutting twelve hundred-weight than they would cutting forty, because in order to cut twelve in a day or even in a morning one has to be really ingenious, devising pretexts for being idle in the cane-fields, piddling around to get out of cutting cane. There are cane-cutters who suddenly get the urge to talk when the time comes to cut cane. It may be said that silence when cutting cane is a good index for measuring the effort being put forth. Talking means a waste of energy, of breath, breaks up your rhythm and dries your gullet. There are cane-cutters who walk three hundred yards looking for a file. Sometimes the file gets lost, and the man responsible for the file never shows up. It is not worth making the sacrifice going to the cane-fields to do that. Really it is not worth the sacrifice. That type of activity makes no sense at all. And here we have the two extremes: the man who talks a blue streak and works as little as possible, and the man who cuts one hundred, one hundred and twenty-five, one hundred and seventy-five hundredweight. The differences are incredible. Rarely can it be said that one man is ten or twenty times as strong as another. Nobody is anxious to admit that another man is ten times as strong as he is, or ten times as tough, or ten times as healthy, given normal health conditions. Maybe someone will admit to another's being two or three times as strong as he, but he will not go so far as to say ten or twenty times as strong. Cane-cutting is undoubtedly hard monotonous work. It is just plain foolishness going to the cane-fields concentrating on this, instead of thinking of what it means, instead of thinking that this is the way to free ourselves from this almost enslaving job, from that hard work. It is out and out stupidity to go if one is not aware of the meaning, of the importance of each stroke of the machete, of each cane cut. And — especially at this time — it makes no sense at all to go to the cane-field if one does not intend to cut cane."

Castro ended up cutting fifty hundredweight in a morning, according to a *Granma* report.

The International *Herald-Tribune* of Tuesday July 28, 1970, headlined a *New York Times* report: CUBAN ECONOMY NEAR CHAOS. CASTRO ASSUMES THE BLAME. Half-way down the first column it became clear that the chaos wasn't endemic in the Cuban economy as the headline implied, but was a severe dislocation resulting from the over-ambitious ten-million-ton harvest. "Mr Castro said that the efforts to produce a record ten-million-ton harvest this year, which failed by about 1·5 million tons, had been disastrous to output in the rest of agriculture and in the fields of industry and services.

"He said that with the exception of a small increase in the ration of rice, fish, and eggs, all other foods and manufactured products received from the Soviet Union were distributed in smaller quantities than before.

"Not only was output lower, but administrative 'irresponsibility' and transportation problems have occasionally stopped production altogether, Mr Castro said.

"He said that in some cases cattle in railroad cars in Havana had not been unloaded for days. Cuban ports are also clogged with merchandise because of the lack of transportation, he said, and even factories that have raw materials have reduced their production to a minimum because of indiscriminate mobilisation of key personnel for agriculture.

"Mr Castro said that labour productivity was low, worker absenteeism high and the quality of Cuban products inferior. He said he had seen shoes that had disintegrated after five days of wear.

" 'The enemy will say our difficulties are growing, and he will be right; the enemy will say we have problems of inefficiency, and he will be right; the enemy will say there is discontent, and he will be right, and we have no fear of admitting it' the premier said."

The ten-million-ton failure was an emotional blow for Fidel, with incalculable political consequences, since it deepens his debt to the Russians. Nonetheless there was a record harvest (8·4 million tons) which in an earlier speech Castro described as a triumph for the people in the cane-fields. He attributed their falling short of ten million tons to the inefficient management of sugar mills, and mentioned the late arrival of vital machinery, some of it from strife-torn Czechoslovakia. He assumed general responsibility for the failure and offered to resign, but most Cubans are so keenly aware of his personal anguish that his standing among them is unshaken. On the other hand there will be disenchantment among the uncommitted, and bitter division in the society. Under these circumstances the door seems to me to be wide open for repressive bureaucratic measures, but what Fidel actually proposed was more say for the workers. Collective leadership would be organized in factories, with workers having as much say as the administrator and the representatives of the Communist Party — the Chinese road, in fact, on Russian money, a tight-rope walk that it will be difficult for Fidel to survive. But *if* over the next few years Cuba can maintain a yearly sugar harvest of eight and a half million tons, worth nearly a billion dollars, this should go far to ensure economic stability.

Perhaps the purely economic effects of the harvest have received too much attention both in Cuba and abroad. Equally important is the fact that the harvest was produced, not by hungry and ignorant wage-slaves working sixteen hours a day for four months and unemployed the rest of the year, but by volunteers who were more politically and culturally aware. This moral currency has, of course, little value, and Castro's survival will depend on hard cash.

I decided to try voluntary labour. The hotel staff were going out on Sundays to work in coffee, so I got up early, joined the people drinking coffee and eating a biscuit in the throaty five o'clock dark, caught a truck that came two hours late. I grumbled, but they all said "Progress, it used to be four hours late," and we drove happily through the Cuban morning. Then I started digging holes in the ground, to fill cellophane bags with earth for the coffee plants, and learnt the art of packing them evenly in rows.

I soon realized that I preferred writing plays, but people round me seemed quite relaxed and I persisted till my back ached. That I could bear, but not the boredom. It all seemed like playing in dirt. Dig and fill, dig and fill; I longed for, watched for, the breaks for cold sugar and water, then lunch. A man shouted gaily "What, no music, no baseball?" Everybody laughed except me. They turned on the damned sound-system. I preached to myself the gospel of work — as revolutionary for the bourgeois, I said, as christianity for the Graeco-Roman aristocracy. My dry dirty paws couldn't grip the chalky cellophane bags; my teeth were on edge, my nerves cringed. I wanted a bath. I thought of delights in far away places, but the sun was insistent. I said to my happy neighbour "People don't write books in order to read them, why should I have to plant coffee to drink it?" I walked three hundred yards for a larger shovel, and wondered what the hell it must be like cutting cane.

"The new man," said the ageing doctor, "is a man who works in agriculture, God bless him, then goes and performs an operation. Of course you might say it won't be a good operation, insufficient practise, too much time in the cane, but all the good surgeons I know used to spend hours on the golf course so why not the cane-fields or driving a bus? There is your classless society. Your equality. No labouring class. Now you will still have brilliant doctors and bad doctors, and that's choking inequality, but choking I fear ends in heaven and we are in Cuba. And of course if people study medicine for love and aptitude, not money and kudos, there'll be fewer charlatans. There will still be unequal talents, you know, and envy. I like to be in charge of something, some programme, but I'm quite satisfied that by and large, by and large mark you, I approve of the medical programme in Cuba; by and large. Nobody quite does anything your way but then neither do you do things their way, so just let the thing be done, so long as it's very broadly correct, it doesn't matter by who.

"And you see, when real work is being done you get less envious of the successful people because they are actually achieving visible things, not just fashionable arse-lickers. I am an able man, I think, an ambitious man; I'm constantly by-passed; I never see Fidel these days. But when I get up in the morning what I think about is the revolution. I don't want to leave this country. Look at Che — you tell me, perhaps, he went to carve out his own empire in Latin America, but surely the *sine qua non* of mere power is to stay alive. He was king here in Cuba. People worshipped Fidel but they loved Che. He carried through the thing that saved this revolution, moral incentives. But he went because he thought individuals have only a relative value. The revolution is all-important. No, man's idealism is strong. Che said to me 'The only way to work with Fidel is to set your mind on the problem, not on who solves the problem. Only the revolution is finally important.' So he left his beloved wife and children. And he never ratted on Fidel. Extraordinary. The bourgeois press wasn't allowed the joy of a murder or a defection. Yet can you imagine what it was like working with Fidel in 1962 when the revolution hit rock bottom? He just kept falling about on people, feeling that he was plagued with fools. He was savage in those years. He cursed people. A very shy, diffident man he is most times, a humble man ready to praise good work, and almost too ready to take advice because really he finds folly unbelievable. How could any expert tell him to go ahead on a scheme unless that expert knew it was right? So he'd go ahead, spend millions, and when nothing happened simply start all over again, sometimes without even sacking the fool, just cursing himself for being naïve. He's always saying he's not a utopian and that's absolutely true, but he's gullible, he doesn't know the bottom of people. But he's learning. In fact now he's gone to the other extreme and simply plays his own hunches, do this, do that, people follow him around with little books and take it all down. But he doesn't ever trust them. He makes his own notes. You're right that he was always stubborn, but he didn't always absolutely trust his own genius and know that nine out of ten people were fools.

"It takes an arrogant man to know that instinctively, and Fidel had to learn it. You want concrete examples of all this? What sort of book are you writing, a low-down on Fidel? Everybody knows about his rages. When free burials were announced the unfortunate announcer cracked a joke that we'd all need them and he got ten years. At the time there was grave threat of counter-revolution and Fidel clamped down. Tyrant? What would have happened to an announcer who did that in England during the war? Cuba is at war. Fidel is no more tyrant than Churchill. D'you know something? Something just occurred to me. How few really serious defections we've had. Consider how long the top boys have all been there. And they aren't fools. Hart isn't a fool. He may be a born follower and too fond of phrases like chain of command but not a fool."

I cut in here because of something I had long wanted to talk about.

"Che in one of his essays," I said, "seems to suggest that some are born to lead and some to follow — a strange kind of aristocracy for a socialist. Have I got it wrong?" (Che's actual words are: "Revolutionary institutions ... permit the natural selection of those who are destined to march in the vanguard, and who dispense rewards and punishments to those who fulfil their duty or act against the society under construction.")

"You must know the background," he said. "Our revolution suffered disastrously from too many people talking. Too many bright young egos complete with ideas. A hundred ideas on what to do with the small farmers, or sugar-workers. Everybody was dizzy and in despair at the end of those early meetings, except of course those who got drunk on talk — the majority, come to think. It was absolutely necessary to cut out the words and have orders from people who had had some sort of success in carrying things through, and others had to obey because after all the individual, whether leader or follower, is only of relative importance. Che believed in natural leaders who emerge and are obeyed because everybody's concern is not who gives or takes orders but the success of a democratic revolution. And of course obedience stops if the revolution is being perverted. When power is as rational as that normal men accept it, don't they? It chokes a bit, men were born to choke, but they accept it.

"Fidel is a good example. In '60-'62 when all this planification was going on — Russian experts with slide rules — Fidel didn't understand a damn thing they were doing. We had a drink and he sat there saying 'fuck planification', but thinking it was all very decisive, so he took a back seat and more or less handed over the country to those who he thought had expertise in organization and planning — old communist theologians like Anibal Escalante who nearly strangled the country in Marxism-Leninism. You know what occurs to me — that theologies belong to societies that pass the time talking — words, words, words, rhythmic words, fine-spun ideas, texts, precedents, heresies, interpretations. They're all priests who don't mean to lift a finger. This business of leadership — decisive. Is it pure luck that we have Fidel? Well in the sense that he might have come later rather than sooner, but the social realities — the need for everybody to eat, for technology to produce this food, for education to provide technologists — keep on pressing and eventually find a leader to answer them, more or less fully. But it's luck as well. Suppose Escalante had been leading Cuba! I suppose we would simply be a Czechoslovakia, clogged up with theology and bankrupt bureaucrats living off the lean of the land, and workers fed up with slide rules that calculate incentive down to the last millimetre. China would be the only hope left for real communism, but of course mandarins are strong there too. Mao is a mandarin fighting mandarins with his little red book. But he works. At least he swims. Yes, the Chinese work. We have misunderstandings with them, but we're much nearer to them than to the Russians. We must trade more with China and less with Europe. We mustn't get dependent on class societies.

"People, of course, say there is a ruling élite in Cuba. Well, yes, in the sense that rulers are always an élite and have certain privileges, but only a fool would fail to consider the degree of privilege. What's important is sharing the dirty work and the food, and by and large we do that here. Once everybody studies, then of course dead-end jobs will have to be shared. Will everybody study, particularly if they don't have to? God knows, but anyway sharing the dirty work is the ideal in this society and in China. It isn't in Europe or Russia. Because it is impracticable? No, no. Our ideals are simply sturdier. And the children will study if they're brought up that way. Their intelligence, perhaps, will vary, but few people can't take any kind of education, if we're careful to put round pegs in round holes, d'you know. Intelligence will vary a little and that's choking, but choking as you know ends in heaven.

"I still choke a little. Before the revolution I never stopped thinking of my career, aching, groaning — ah there, you say, that's like you. You say that's exactly like you. Well, it's like everybody. I feel my talents aren't being used but then I console myself that I can play rather a lot of chess. I couldn't do that if I was a minister. I play a lot of chess when I feel like it — I daren't tell you how much. My chief service to this glorious revolution is not to gripe. I do my bit in the fields. I'm not happy because I'm a worrier, but I manage. Chess leaves me deeply satisfied. And all round me in Cuba things are being done that answer my dreams. You say that sounds like happiness. All right."

One Sunday morning I went to a party given by this old doctor, where, he told me, Major G was expected. The doctor was a little drunk, wisps of hair standing up instead of smoothed over his baldness. Major G was coming. He said it five times in the next two hours to arriving guests. To a guest who was leaving he said, "If you wait, Major G's coming, he may give you a lift." The Major was a comforting proof of nearness to the throne, a sign of grace. The doctor's was clearly still a revolutionary house, visited by the brass. No matter that he spent Sunday drinking black-market rum, he still had face. He who had thrown bombs wasn't slipping. Major G, a right hand of Fidel, was coming. This booze-up could almost count as a conference, a putting together of heads, a comparing of notes. The other guests were unimportant old friends, one or two of them counted slightly, but they weren't names that appeared in *Granma*. Major G was redemptive.

Major G never came. At about four the doctor's sensible wife, not giving a damn about Major G so long as she had her husband and the house and went on eating, served what food there was. Friends had brought their offerings, and everybody had a mouthful. A young wife giggled that the Major probably foresaw the lunch, and her husband, choking with laughter, snorted food through his nose. An upper-class girl said the really important people in Cuba were the mechanics who came to service the telly or fridge, and included the mistress as well. The doctor's wife made little treks to a secret supply of rum which she brought to her husband.

I talked to him late in the afternoon, when the Havana light was saddening and he was totally, tiredly drunk, sitting with eyes shut, and aching with humiliation.

"It looks," he said to his wife, "as if Major G isn't coming." She glanced at me, checking how much of the scene I dug. This man was an early revolutionary, had talked endless nights about how to get the Yankees out of Cuba, had actually thrown bombs. And now Major G who threw nothing . . . didn't even come.

A slender little bitch joined us. Stroking him fondly, she began to reminisce.

"I miss the real Havana. I miss my youth. Dressing up on a Saturday morning, oh my God, and shopping. All week I sit in the office typing, going over in my mind what to buy. If you have no money, well you window shop, no?" He wasn't listening. She went on, "I want to buy, buy, buy. There used to be such hundreds of things. Pick, choose, refuse. What stockings to buy, what lipstick to use, which magazine to browse in, whether to go to the beach or the hotel swimming-pool. Shops had such hundreds of choices. Your eyes, your life, fed on such beautiful things like — like everything — things you would never dream of buying like tyres, tools, trucks, day-old chicks. Freedom is this ordinary everyday choice — where to travel, when, who with, whether to have breakfast, what to have.

If you weren't shopping in shops you were shopping in magazines, or as you typed at the office. It was such a free life."

She sat on the arm of the doctor's chair touching the lids of his shut eyes. "And you would space out the shopping you know, perfume this week — a long trek all round before you buy a bottle you'd set your heart on long before. Sandals next week. Next few weeks you're flat broke except for buying your magazine. But of course what they say is true — if everybody was shopping and eating and travelling, all that choice would immediately — the coach would really turn into a pumpkin, no? It was truly a freedom for the few, and what they say we are making in Cuba is a freedom for the masses. So there will be lines and shortages, perhaps for a long time, perhaps for ever like in Russia. Of course I used to distrust the masses — lazy people. Only lazy people would live as they lived; any young man, young girl, with drive would get up and go. And of course many did — into prostitution and crime. Or they got so fed up with failing — I realize now they just worked and worked and what did they see? The servant in my house worked from seven till six, then had eight children to go home and look after. And there I was all my life thinking, lazy people. That's a typical bourgeois conscience, no?"

The doctor interrupted her: "When are you leaving, Dolly?"

"Tomorrow. So it's goodbye."

She embraced him fondly and left to join her aunt in New York.

He held my hand. "The envy in a small country," he said, "is concentrated. People go and live abroad to escape it."

I told him that just after I left school a friend of mine was going abroad to study and I went to see him off. I was invited to go and have a look inside the aeroplane and I refused, vowing to myself that the first time I went inside an aeroplane would be when I was flying away in one. And I could see that for certain people to live in Cuba — or worse, Havana, which is still Cuba, a tight little place where you know the ruling circle but despair . . . He glanced round scathingly at his guests and said nothing. Silence.

"What was that you said?" I was waiting my chance to talk

politics again. His wife distrusted this and had kept us apart, but now she'd given up — he could say what he liked and I could quote him, who cared. He looked malevolently across at a man who had written a book but still hadn't quite made it. "You see the Cuban is a born bureaucrat. Put a pen in his hand and he's arrived. The real revolutionary wants to be out there in the field dragging up the rice by its ear."

There were a few young people there. They sang, *Cuba, beautiful Cuba.* Grandmother clapped. Two of them were holding hands in the two-car garage which was empty. Dusty old golf-clubs stood in a corner — there were chickens now on the eighteenth green. The doctor pressed himself up, belching and farting, his face bitter with indigestion — a different man. He said thoughtfully, "The real trouble is that Fidel is a paid-up member of the rat-race, a born contender. Nothing to do with equality. He only went communist to crap on the Yankees. He's a revengist. And here in Cuba equality applies — well equality applies to me, to you, but not him and his."

Sylvia, the black girl I'd come to the party with, heard this and winked at me. She usually liked taking people up on things, but she left him alone and walked out into the street. I had met her through people on the block I had cased. She was a sort of in-law of the embittered hurricane Mrs S, whose son George had fathered a child on her, long ago, before the revolution. It was through her and her friends that I saw something of the colour set-up in Cuba. I joined her in the street and asked her to tell me about George.

Sylvia said, "I went to Mrs S's house, her white house, the house she lived in then; it wasn't all that posh or big, but to me it seemed to float. It's like the way you think of the States when you're a child — unreal. This ordinary house, these damn useless people, yet they were gods in a temple — imagine! That woman with her bad varicose veins! These were white people. I was sleeping with her son, but that didn't make him any realer. The bed was at my mother's shop, in the back. My mother and I slept in it. When my grandmother came my mother slept on the counter in the shop, and I

slept with Granny in the bed. She was asleep and he crept in and
we were on the floor which was nearly falling in. He wanted to
open the door to let the moon in so he could see me. He caressed me
as if he really loved me, but I didn't dare to hold him. He was a soft
white man and I would do anything for him — work for him, lie
down for him, have a baby for him, but I didn't dare to hold him.

"I loved him. He wasn't the kind of young white Cuban who
would pass and put his hand on your front. That kind of brute I
could deal with. But George would hang around feeling very
romantic — till the sperm was out of his sack of course, and then
he was off. Days he would pass the shop and forget I was there.
Then he'd way-lay me at night, push me up against a tree then down
on the ground, and curl up on my body like a baby. Then he would
be very anxious, and I never felt I could hold him.

"I am a woman who feels her rights, from very young; for
example I knew where black men stood with me. I was reserved for
white. Then when I was pregnant and never saw George, he wasn't
even passing the shop, my mother made me go to see Mrs S. I went
through the side gate but right onto the verandah, she was sitting
in the dining-room, and I passed boldly through the drawing-room,
and it was like I told you — the house was afloat. It wasn't absolutely steady on the ground. I could make out a piano, but the mother
and the grandmother seemed wavy white people. George was there
in the back yard fixing some car — he's still working as a mechanic.
I gave her a note I'd written down, and she said, 'What is this? Go
away.' The grandmother just sighed. She knew. So I went away
and Mrs S said, 'This damn bitch comes into my dining-room!'

"So I took a bus to where my aunt lived and had the baby. My
great-aunt. Left the baby with her and went back to the shop. I
never went back to the baby, then one day George was there in a
car and kidnapped the baby. My aunt, frantic, came to the shop.
She went to that house and kicked up shit and Mrs S phoned the
police who dragged her away. When she fought them they dragged
her along the ground, and she was sixty. She was bursting and
covered in blood, and wouldn't wash it off, just got on the bus and

went home. So there was me at the shop and my baby not far down the road. The only thing I felt was against Mrs S calling the police, and even that didn't come much into focus. Now with my eyes wide open by the revolution I think of all that and no revenge is possible. I just feel they can never pay for any of that. I think of my aunt and close my eyes.

"Well, as I tell you, my child was down the road, and when he was six the revolution sent me back to school to get sixth grade. I had no grade, practically. I was twenty. Really I came to life with the literacy campaign. I went out to teach. The thought of going to the deep country was exciting. I kept on thinking what I would need and all I could think of was soap, for some reason. When I got to the region — the journey was terrible. There was a mix-up about where to sleep, and we ended up sleeping cold on the road. One young boy just started walking back home. Never asked any question or looked back. I lay there wondering what real mountain peasants who didn't even know money would be like — absolutely certain I'd teach them to read and write, teach them, teach them, cram it down them like medicine down a sick hog's throat. When I got there and they saw me they ran and hid, and I sat there like a fixture till night came, then morning, then the next night, starving and very cold, but calmly waiting to teach every last one of those Cubans to read. And it was while I was sitting there that I decided that I would get my son back, and that he wasn't going to leave Cuba with that family of *gusanos*. If my son was still there when I got back, he wouldn't leave Cuba.

"Outside this revolution black people have a funny sort of life. Your father was chopped up, my father was a policeman who bought the shop and bar on crookedness and was stabbed to death; one of your uncles is a half-lunatic without a roof of his own; one of mine was a criminal till the revolution let him out. Is there any black family not acquainted with this kind of misery? We take it for granted. And other people take it for granted that we are used to it — as your play says, 'cook the food we can't eat, wash the clothes we can't wear, and make the bed we can't climb into and sleep'. That was mostly the position here before the revolution, and now of course Cuban blacks still complain that we are over-represented in sport and under-represented in the government. Afro-Cubans read *Granma* and there is a big page regularly, in colour, about African culture, but certain Afro-Cubans were excluded from our famous cultural conference because the Government didn't want their reflections on the racial set-up in Cuba. And what is the racial set-up? Well, we all get the same education but since blacks used to be at the bottom there is still a cultural lag and proportionately more black children drop out. Some Afro-Cubans want a special government effort to push black children, but the Government believes that these things will right themselves, so long as it rigorously enforces a law on compulsory education right up to university level. Cuba is twenty-five per cent black and the Government wants no kind of racial issue. They don't want to pass the word that where a black can be promoted he must be given preference. The schools are there for everybody, the hotels. There is no public racism. But a lot of private racism, because Cuba used to be like the American south. In the parks in Santa Clara blacks walked one side and whites another. Batista was a tame mulatto and there were a few others like him, but they were kept out of the exclusive clubs. So now there is the hangover. People are all just recently down from the trees, and our heads are full of rocks and regions that kill. Full of memories that kill. Aggressive. And of course we need aggression to live.

"When I entered medical school I went out with a white boy who kept telling me how to behave, and whose father, a revolutionary, approved of me because the coupling would 'improve the race'. Our children would be whiter than me. He mentioned that old shit in my hearing, in a sadistic sort of way, and the fellow-revolutionary he said it to winked at him. Right in my face. It was on that business I broke with the son. He saw what happened same as me, and would not admit it. Would not admit, because really at bottom he wasn't all that upset about it. He didn't hate it. My ex-husband is a black man, in a good job, and his habit in his office is to remain seated in an easy-going sort of way and ask visitors to sit, but the other day a

Spaniard walked in and he *unconsciously* stood up, then explained it away, to me. But still these are new days for blacks in Cuba. We are still the drop-outs but we are not exactly dragged on the ground."

A few weeks later I found George, who was still repairing cars and lived in the country, a confidently ignorant white man, who liked his job. I asked him about Sylvia and their son.

"1961 was full of all these communistic interferences, and I knew it would never get better. It was getting worse and worse my dear sir, and it would never get better. And my mother knew very substantial people in the United States; there would be no trouble about going there. I could always find work, yesterday, today, tomorrow, as long as Mr Ford's invention exists. I was very well assured that I could look after my son and my mother. The boy is coloured but his grandmother had no doubts about how her friends up there would react. I had doubts. You never can tell — strangers, you understand — the boy is coloured, would that put gum in the works, ha, ha, now I wasn't sure, but the grandmother had no doubts, and she of course knew substantial people.

"So then all of a sudden the boy's mother . . . The first thing we knew was interference from these new officials, telephone conversations with these scarcely literate people, letters — let me go from the first blow.

"I was out in the front fixing a vehicle, the boy was helping me, and a government agent, a communist agent, came up, this complete stranger, and started telling me things. This is communism. My hands were greasy. I wanted to cuff him. He had a gun but I would have cuffed him if my hands weren't greasy. The grandmother came out because she can scent things happening, she saw all this coming long ago, and there was this agent saying what could be done and what could not be done. So the long and the short was I had every intention of leaving Cuba with my family through unusual channels. It would cost money but I was making my share. The vehicles were all falling to bits, like the country, and I was in them, under them, on top of them day and night making a lot of money, with my little boy helping me — staying at home, we wouldn't send him to their various schools. No, my mother taught him here at home very efficiently. I must say that about my mother, anything she does, very efficient, and I am like her in that. My grandfather was like that, and it came down through the female to me. What my son will be like now . . . it must be my sin. Some sin of mine. The boy was mine, had no dealings with his mother, none whatsoever, a little black girl in a bar — he didn't even know that. There were many times I thought of moving because I believed people round here would shame him with that, but they respect us too much. They say nothing about the mother. There have been one or two damn careless remarks, and the boy is alert, but nothing much. He never knew her. That class of person could never be in his life, till this government exposed him.

"I confess to you that at this stage of the game I made a mistake. When the usual channels weren't open I should have realized that numerous agents would be on the alert about our leaving in other ways. And once they found that out they claimed the child was in danger and must be boarded out at one of their various schools. There was this hell boiling in me to shoot it out, and my mother — you can imagine — asthma, which she'd never had for years, and losing weight fighting the case, and my grandmother was the only one to tell the child what was happening. She told him we were sending him to school, and he went into a silence. He was close to me. So I told him about the mother, that she was an ignorant woman who I could never introduce him to and that she was responsible for all this, and he said that no matter how much they taught him he would never learn anything. So I sent him off a little more satisfied.

"We were all condemned to this Cuban prison sentence. My mother just got desperate and started shouting at me that I must get a boat, that if I was a real man I would get a boat — things like that. She would accept no explanations, my dear sir, saying was I so afraid of prison, what sort of man was I, Castro was better than me. All this, morning, noon and night. We would eat without her looking at me. She wouldn't accept the explanation that we were too closely watched to move. To enter into any serious negotiation would be impossible. I didn't mind prison so much for me, but for her. She wouldn't believe that. She said I was a coward and left the house. She never mentions me any more, or her grandson, or any part of that story. Once she left the house the boy stopped coming home at all."

I asked him whether he was impressed with anything the Government had done, and he said Batista was gradually achieving all this without taking away people's property. "What is so wrong about freedom? There were bad conditions, well of course, people are lazy, live in *bohios* (slums), all that, but that is not very serious. Sickness, yes, but a person can quite well live in a *bohio*, pick up a little food here and there sometimes in a very bareface way — they used to come into my yard and stone the fruit-trees, climb them and pick all they want — a person can live in a *bohio* and have the pleasure of not working and not need very much to carry on. The sun is hot, you don't even strictly speaking need a room. Nobody in Cuba was starving. Undernourished, well, but those men were stronger than you and me — and the women could work hard in the house. Not that they weren't damn lazy and drifted about. They live very long, till God knows when, and if any of them have ambition — instead of jigging outside the bar they could come down here and learn to fix a car, and then they wouldn't have to live in a *bohio*. No, things were never too bad in Cuba. Everybody lived how they wanted to live. Bread was cheap, and rice and beans."

I showed him a *Granma* photograph of pre-revolutionary housing, with the following account of the conditions.

"Their room is narrow and dark. It has no windows. Cave-like, it has only a single entrance. Here, tripping all over each other, lived Delia, her son, her mother, three orphaned nieces, a brother who had gone crazy, and a tubercular sister. The tenement building consists of sixteen rooms — for sixteen families. There are two toilets for the whole building, and they are located in front of Delia's room. The stench is overpowering. Tears come to Delia's eyes as she recalls her little sister Lilia. As she coughed her life out in the final stages of tuberculosis, the saddened family took to sleeping outside, under the flimsy protection of the doorway or in the open. Two sick people in the narrow dark room; seven hungry mouths. And only Delia's fifteen dollars a month maid's salary to sustain them. And theirs was not an isolated case; poverty and sadness surrounded them. In every room the situation was the same. 'I can still see the belongings of Hemenegilda Cuesta piled in the middle of the yard,' said Delia Abreau. 'When it stormed a river ran right through her room; it rained harder inside than out. She refused to pay the rent — she wanted to use the money to fix the roof — and Leandro, the landlord threw all her things out into the yard. Hemenegilda was forced to pay the rent, carry everything back into the room, and put up with the rain.' "

George smiled as he looked at the newspaper, the photographs, and said, "Hemenegilda, what a name, these people certainly have names. And there was a lot of manpower in that little room. You have to look at all these things not as in a newspaper, but in the way it really goes. The three nieces could be earning if they weren't too young. They don't say how young. It sounds like mother, grandmother, sick sister, crazy brother, and four children. Well usually the sick sister and crazy brother wouldn't be sick or crazy and they would be working. They wouldn't have to live in these places. Of course I know, well, clearly people do live in these places, not so much in Cuba but in Mexico, all those countries and even in this Cuban tenement you will notice, I believe I am right, that only one room has the stench. But of course they choose to tell people about *that* room, to fool the people with the crazy brother and sister. They are what you would call a special case. But not everybody would know about special cases, the concept of special cases. And this Hemenegilda — Hemenegilda — my God ... You see the rain flooded into *her* room. A special case. There were sixteen rooms. The rain flooded over into *her* room. But they take this thing called the special case to fool people about conditions in Cuba. And of course these places still exist. These people seem to be only just moving after how many years of revolution, and how many promises of housing. Private enterprise would have pulled these places down long ago and provided cheap housing for anybody who wanted it. Clearly wherever there are sufficient needs it pays private enterprise to build houses in conditions of freedom. No need for any revolution to rob people. To make decent people join the crowd.

"You could never get me to go and work anywhere as one of a crowd. Not unless they send me to prison. You think anybody could send me to work in a big garage with scores of black people, taking orders? This government, Castro, closed down all the one-man businesses, thousands of them. Now what is going to happen to all these people — industrious people? They send them to agriculture to work in gangs. If they wanted to be one of a crowd they could be lazy and live in a tenement like Hemenegilda. But they open a business. You think anybody could send me to work in a gang? I would die laughing. I am very lucky. I can still make a living of my own because this new class of people have cars that need quick fixing and if they send them to the State garages they wait one year to the next. They go in and never come out. A friend of mine was a dry-cleaner, ran the place himself with his family, why close that down? Castro called them parasitic; they don't dig the fields so they mustn't eat food — well that is ridiculous. They work till late into the night, those people, and they make a lot of money, why? Because they serve a need. Castro says they spend their money buying black-market pork — well stop the black-market if you like, but a man needs his business. Not to take orders from anybody. This friend of mine — no, they didn't knock him about or insult him, he couldn't complain about that, there was nothing rough, so to speak rough, but he's in agriculture for six months, without his family, and God knows where after that. They give a dry-cleaner a job in agriculture. All right, somebody must dig the fields, but let the people who love the soil do that. The farmers round here were poor, not here so much as round our old country place, very poor, ate beans and weak coffee, but they loved their beans and loved the soil. That's why Castro had to leave those people alone. He dared not lock up those people on a State farm. Now, my friend will never get used to it out there in the country. Not even a bathroom. You eat with the plate on your lap. Sleep in a tent with other people. His only privacy is his suitcase, and when he gets up in the morning he is not his own man. He stands round helpless waiting for orders. I don't want him there. I would vote against that. Mario standing round waiting for orders out there in the wilderness, no wife, no family. The man came here to see me and he was in tears. He didn't know why. But I know why. Because he is a dry-cleaner, used to town, to his wife and family, not used to all those damn black people in the same tent. It is terrible. But he doesn't want to go away and leave his son here with the State. And it would take him time to get away. So his life is in ruins. And he didn't choose it that way. The blasted Hemenegilda and her flood chose it that way. And they are in the minority, you see. Less people live in the tenements than in houses. How many people were unemployed in Batista Cuba? About half a million? As much as that? I would say no. Genuinely unemployed, well thousands. Not half a million. Anyway, well, half a million and you say another one million under-employed. Well one and a half million out of seven million is a great minority. Well yes, and their families, the poorest have the biggest, all right say families of five — grandmother, old aunt, no, no, not the grandfather, the grandfather is usually dead — old aunt and a few children; of course there are families of eighteen and twenty — the old boy never stops clucking — but those are special cases. Well say five dependents, that is one and a half million times five, well according to you nearly the total population was in straits, but that can never be true. How can that be true? They would outvote Batista. Batista would have lost every election long ago. These figures are from special sources."

Castro says that prejudice against blacks and women facilitates their economic exploitation, and will end when there is no more exploitation. Certainly, judging by the usual standards of wages and social facilities, Cuba is no longer a racist, sexist country, and in our world this is a tremendous achievement. Traditional attitudes shift slowly, however, so that blacks and women are still far from being fairly represented in the Cuban government. One can easily find quite young people, like Sylvia's son, bitter with prejudice.

I spent a long time trying to find this boy, who was at school in yet another part of the country. He was sober for a seventeen-year-old, very deliberate — exactly like his mother whom he'd never met. I found myself gingerly keeping my distance.

He told me: "All the time I was at school I was a counter-revolutionary. I planned to join the rebels. I did my lessons and got regular promotion, so did the teachers know what I really felt? Some of them couldn't even talk decent Spanish. They would say about miners taking over the mines in Bolivia and I would learn it but make a mental note that I'd check with my grandmother. I'm surprised that I didn't allow any of my problems to get in the way of lessons. I just planned counter-revolution, and did the work. Then the first crisis of my life came when they asked me what I wanted to do after I got sixth grade. I said counter-revolutionary and the man said he knew all about that, then we talked about my family and for the first time I heard my mother's side of the story. I was very impressed with how much these agents knew. He talked and talked and all I could think was 'black woman, black woman, black woman'.

"He must have thought I was crying about her and said did I want to meet her and I said very haughtily, 'I don't think that sort of meeting would be appropriate.' I wrote and told my grandmother all about it but of course didn't expect to hear from her. I'm sure I never heard from her because they intercepted her letters. [His father had said she never wrote.] After this I stopped working, loafed, played the fool, read Yankee comics that were passed round secretly. So I failed sixth grade twice. I didn't even care about going home. Whenever I got home I just ate a lot of black-market goodies that my great-grandmother had saved up, and worked with my father. Once I passed the shop where *my* mother used to work. I thought 'such a life'. When my great-grandmother died I kept seeing myself in the coffin. It was very pleasant. I went to army-school, I thought yes, forced labour, after all I was a prisoner in Cuba. I thought, I'll go quietly, knowing all. I'll just suffer quietly, because that's life.

"I was on this great kick about night. Night was my season, the most precious thing in my life. I expected all the stupid orders and obeyed them; played baseball, enjoying it, because I was really dead and buried with my great-grandmother, obsessed, like worms in my head — long worms swallowing short fat worms then swallowing her but she was still there. I became so good at motions they found me promising. I got grade six. I decided the thing I wanted most was to be a tractor driver, and found myself laughing at what my grandmother would think, then realized I was laughing against her. I thought two things — of her phoning the police; and that it would be interesting to meet my real mother. But that wasn't serious and there it ended.

"Driving a tractor made me a worker. I hardly study. I am a worker, a soldier — same thing. They talk about me being a model worker but I don't accept the name. In my heart I accept no titles from this revolution. I drive tank and tractor, I am a worker, a soldier. I have no desire at all to see my family and I wish the revolution well. I am a mulatto, a negro, a black working man. My friends are black working men. I'm happy with them. I have very few feelings about women. And white Cubans I dislike. Any whity who tells me he feels equal with a black Cuban is a liar. My revenge is to have minimum dealings with them. Polite. No more. One of my hobbies is to watch black men climb up in the revolution. That is my only interest in the revolution. I want a negro to succeed Castro, but of course the whites . . . you know . . . they will succeed him. One thing, they can't make me study. That's one thing they definitely can't do. No, negroes are workers. Not farmers, not bureaucrats, not students, but workers. Castro must be content with that. Perhaps if you could study happiness I'd study."

He had backed into the revolution through a side-door and I wondered where he would end. His grandmother had given him up, he had given up his father, and his mother was afraid to meet him — "too many problems".

One of the people I met at the doctor's party was a farmer who was fretting about his house — a large house apparently, with an old servant. I met him again later. "Castro," he said, "has that flair, doesn't he — of taking things away from people? Look at Cuba, my dear man, the Americans, the middle class, the Vatican — all robbed. My God, how did he do it, and what chance have I got with my house? It'll be my turn next. These private houses are next on the list — one room per person, per student. Think of the Americans as solid as God above us, and Cuba is now communist. He's worked it all out. First he divided Batista from the middle classes and crushed Batista. Then he turned on the middle classes while he larded the servant-girls with stockings, gave the small farmers more land, and the small traders promises of security. Then it was the turn of the masses. He starved them while the small farmers and traders still had it good. Now he's finished off the traders and the small farmers grow what he wants. It'll be my house next. He's a man of soft words and hard deeds, that bastard. Young man, the power — only ninety miles away. All those great oil-drums. Oil installations. They belonged to the United States. Huge installations, marked Texaco. All gone. How did it happen? So many gunmen have made their bid like Castro, and nothing happened. Sometimes I wake up at night in a daze, looking round the room for old times."

We went into his house. He became terribly irritable, grinding his teeth and calling his housekeeper for water. He swallowed it and called out to her to take back the glass. The old slave simply did as he said.

"I wish it all wouldn't happen. I live so peacefully in this house."

The twenty thousand Cuban small farmers and their families, who make up more than ten per cent of the population, own roughly forty-three per cent of the best land — running farms of up to 165 acres and earning as much as 20,000 pesos a year (1 peso officially = 1 US dollar). This is far more than anybody else in Cuba earns, except perhaps the 709 doctors still in private practice (working, some of them, part-time in State hospitals). It is certainly far more than anybody in the public sector. A cabinet minister, for example, earns 800 a month. The minimum old-age pension is 60 pesos a month, which is enough to buy all that is obtainable on the ration book. The minimum wage is 80 pesos a month. Cane-cutters earn 96 a month. Intermediate technicians 150–200, young engineers and doctors around 300. There's no taxation, housing is usually free, and the only people who have a hard time buying the meagre rations are families where the husband earns, say, 150 and neither wife nor children work. Better-off people either put their money in a drawer or use it for expensive restaurants or black-market food sold by the small farmers.

Fidel's handling of these farmers is one of the most brilliant strokes of the revolution. On May 17, 1959, in the First Agrarian Reform six months after the triumph of the revolution, he confiscated all holdings over a thousand acres, turned most of them into large State-owned co-operatives (later State farms) to avoid the dangers of fragmentation, but kept down revolt by giving some of the holdings to landless peasants. So genuine sharecroppers who thirsted for land were given land, but people like cane-cutters were regarded as rural proletariat, migrant wage-earners, and continued to earn wages as State employees without serious coercion or open rebellion. Many of them, in fact, drifted to easier jobs in town.

But the confiscation of the largest holdings, which included sugar estates and US property, still left some pretty large holdings in the hands of a few farmers. Eleven thousand farmers, and their families, about one per cent of the population, owned over twenty-five per cent of the land — and seemed a serious counter-revolutionary threat in a country that was soon to be invaded and was already threatened by bands in the Escambray mountains armed by the CIA. Fidel passed the Second Agrarian Reform in 1960, confiscating all holdings larger than 165 acres. Those farmers who elected to stay in Cuba were allowed to live rent-free in their old houses and were given life-time pensions of up to 600 pesos a month. The newly landed peasants who had worked for these men were on the whole very happy with the new reform and Fidel could count on them to defend the revolution.

It is these peasants who now make up the majority of Cuban small farmers. The decision to leave them their land although they produce less than the State farms; to give them more land when their plots were too small; to allow their land to be inherited by one child (though not to be sold except to Government); to let them sell up to twenty-five pounds weight of produce on an open black-market without any interference (except a rationing of petrol blamed on the Russians); to bribe them with houses, loans, equipment to grow what they want (although there's a saying among them that it's either *cana* or *canona*, cane or cannon); this all seems a fairly obvious policy. But another kind of Castro might, after clearing the Escambray of terrorists, have used force to turn them into State farmers and gaoled the rebels. Of course he still has his eye on the land, but his strategy is to make the State farms so efficient that neither the Government nor the public will need to buy the small farmers' produce and they'll all have to sell out to the State — particularly as farm labourers will be impossible to find and as their own children, brought up in technological schools, will understand the virtues of large-scale farming. Already some socialist farmers are selling. Many not so socialist are afraid that in spite of Castro's repeated assurances, he'll seize the land. It must seem to any little *kulack* unnatural to remain so privileged in Cuba for so long, though of course they see nothing wrong in being privileged. After all before the revolution they worked so hard and so long for so little.

It isn't only the privilege mentality that dies hard in Cuba, but even the old slave-mentality. I asked Roberto, a black thirty-five-year-old crane-driver, whether he was going to listen to Castro's big speech on January 2, 1969, and he said, "I have to do what he says anyway, so why should I bother to listen to him? No beer, no clothes. In the last few years I've lost thirty pounds. I used to do this same job for the Americans, I'd have two beers with lunch and go home and have three or four with steak. Dress up and go out to a night-club."

"But everybody wasn't eating then. The farm-labourers who grew the food weren't eating."

"Yes, everybody has now, I know that. I don't complain. I'm not a parasitic man."

"Do you work as hard now as with the Americans?"

"With them it was long hours overtime, whenever the work was there — so long that you got tired. Once I dozed off and smashed a truck. They were good people, the company. They gave me a rest, and said I could come back. I got a good job as a chauffeur with some rich white people — Cubans. The agent for *Reader's Digest*. A uniform went with the job, and now I don't even have clothes. But really I've been a crane-operator all my life and I feel tired. I tried to get something else the other day. On the wharf. I like the smell. But they need me on the crane. They don't want to let me go. But something will turn up and I'll go."

"Can they stop you?"

"No, they say this and that and try to hold onto you."

"What do they say?"

"That my children benefit."

"That's true, isn't it?"

"Yes, but that's another thing now, you see, sometimes I do a night shift, I come home, jump into bed with my wife and want to sleep late with her, but she has to get up to send them to school because she say if they don't go to school the CDR will be down on her. But then if I can't lie in, what am I working for? Next thing they'll be down on the wife to work because they need women for labour. We couldn't use the money, yet she must work. So then who'll cook my food? I tell her not to go."

"The only reason you don't need the money is that you don't have to pay rent and school-fees and doctor's bills."

"I am not a parasitic man."

"Would you leave Cuba?"

"Well yes, because anywhere I am I have to work."

"Are you actually trying to leave?"

"If you could help me."

"But are you trying now?"

"No, I don't think I will ever leave. My wife likes what is happening here. Perhaps soon there'll be more beer and the night clubs will be open. You think so?"

"But if you'd had these four children before the revolution, could you go to night-clubs?"

"Now and again, but there was plenty beer, and the children would soon be out working. At twelve years old I was working!"

The woman who did my room in the hotel came in. I asked her how many eggs she got a week and she looked me dead in the eyes and said, twelve.

"No, not your whole family," I said; "you personally. How many eggs?"

She asked how many we got in Jamaica. "Any amount, if you can afford them."

"But poor people," she said, "can't afford them?"

"No."

She wheeled triumphantly round the room: "There are no poor men in Cuba!"

When I arrived in Havana I stayed for a few weeks at the Havana Libre — formerly the Hilton. It was well kept and full of Cuban workers and students, black and white, obviously a great contrast to what it used to be — the preserve of rich white North American tourists. Yet that same night I was reading an account of Cuba in the English *Sunday Times* by a novelist, and what had struck her about the hotel was one cockroach. No doubt she did see a cockroach (there were none in my room) but there was so much else to see as well. What I wondered was whether the idea of *equality* struck sparks any longer in the great white western psyche. Perhaps all that went out with the barricades, and the lust these days was for meritocracy, the palpitations of making it, the feeling that life was travelling through the creamy-dreamy magazine world and being among the few that arrived.

A close-up of the economic struggle

Next to sugar, cattle-breeding is most important in Cuba's agricultural economy. One of the main centres for cattle research is the Institute of Animal Science, run till 1969 by an Englishman, Doctor Thomas Preston, world-famous for his work on the feeding of molasses and urea to cattle. Doctor Malcolm Willis, another Englishman, was his chief assistant. In January 1969 Doctor Preston told me that Cuba was faced with failure in her cattle-industry — ten per cent of the cattle dying because of feed problems and overgrazing, and little prospect of meat or milk for many years to come. This, he said, was largely the result of wrong-headed direction by Castro who set up as an expert and imposed ignorant policies. Doctor Willis was equally critical. He told me he thought the only hope for Cuba would be if Castro was assassinated.

In his speech of January 2, 1969, in the Plaza de la Revolucion, celebrating the tenth anniversary of the Cuban revolution, Fidel, explaining milk-rationing and other shortages said:

"In a class society the mirage of full store windows created for the masses the illusory idea that all that was necessary was to break the glass and distribute the riches. But the mirage was based on misery, on unemployment and underemployment ... When you divide among eight million people the production created by that type of society, even the second-graders discover that it was a production of misery. When eighty or ninety per cent of the children don't drink milk, 50,000 cows are enough, and there's extra milk in the stores. But when you give milk to all children born in this country, and everyone, without exception, has this right, then 50,000 cows aren't enough, nor 100,000, nor 200,000, but we need half a million. Half a million cows are now growing in this country, and other half millions will be born, and there'll be a quart a day not only for the children but for all citizens of this country at a date not distant.

"At the beginning [of the revolution] our production did not grow — it decreased ... Production went down to 3.8 million tons of sugar. But now it has changed. In Latin America agricultural production goes up one, two or three per cent per year — sometimes less than the population growth. But in Cuba, production in 1970 will be double that in 1958. Something absolutely extraordinary. Unprecedented. Actually this doubling will have been achieved [not in ten years but] in only four or five years. We are learning not only to add but to multiply."

When I asked Doctor Preston whether production in the cattle industry had doubled he said, "Investment has doubled no doubt, but production, if anything, has fallen." These completely different assessments of what ought to be measurable facts reveal some of the technical and — more important — psychological problems that Cuba has often faced in her dealings with foreign advisers, and reflect similar problems in her relations with the United States. I got the Preston/Willis side of the picture when I talked to them in Cuba in January 1969. Fidel stated his own case in his closing speech at the International Congress of the Institute of Animal Science in Havana on May 17, 1969 (reported in *Granma* the following day).

Before the revolution most Cubans didn't eat meat or drink milk, and there was very little knowledge of scientific farming. In 1965 the Institute of Animal Science was set up with Preston at its head. But in the meantime Fidel had made an absolutely crucial decision: the whole country must have milk. How? The five million or so cows in Cuba were chiefly Zebu, which produce next to no milk or meat. There were only a few herds of dairy cows, Holsteins. "How are we going to solve the problem of milk in this country," asked

Fidel, "if we don't have dairy cows? You might answer: well, we have to wait till the dairy cows we have now multiply — that is, wait for the Greek calends — and meanwhile import milk. Or you might answer: let's import hundreds of thousands of pure-bred Holstein cows. This country has imported as many pure-bred cows as possible. There are certain limiting factors — the matter of resources. But even if we had the resources, this country cannot buy cows just anywhere because the blockade is a reality. This country can purchase cattle in very few places. They must be transported by ships — specially conditioned ships — and they must be acclimatized, with all the problems that this involves. However, some years we have imported, through enormous effort, up to two or three thousand head of cattle. But we are not going to solve our problems this way. It is necessary to find another solution" (May 17, 1969).

His solution was to cross Zebu cows with Holstein bulls. After rough and ready experiments he decided that the cross-bred animal, the F.1, would survive Cuban conditions and produce enough milk. "They were," he said, "not strictly controlled tests on a scientific level, but they were tests involving the crossing of a sufficient number of animals, and they were tested under our feeding conditions and the results were observed." On the basis of these results Fidel, who had begun studying genetics, became priest and prophet of a vast programme of cross-breeding and artificial insemination, training thousands of technicians. As a result Cuba now has half a million grade-dairy cattle (F.1s) "which will increase milk production four-fold" (Fidel).

Preston arrived in 1965, after the programme was under way, and challenged its basic premise. Why produce milk? It would be far more profitable for Cuba to produce beef cattle. Fidel answered that profit was not important. The revolution, out of necessity, produced certain things like sugar-cane for profit, but most things for use, regardless of profit.

This disregard of money and profit is fundamental to the revolution. Many Cubans are performing fantastic feats of work without much concern for money. Since they are receiving freely from society — they pay little or no rent, no doctors' bills, no school fees or telephone charges, no taxes, only token bus fares, and not much for food — they give more and more freely. Overtime pay is being increasingly ignored. As a result of this incredible release of energy Fidel claims that agricultural production in most areas — sugar, rice, citrus fruit, coffee, eggs, vegetables — is being doubled, tripled, or even quadrupled by 1970. The dairy herds are growing rapidly. A psychology of inevitable abundance has developed, that dispenses with too much book-keeping. Money is regarded as an economic bottleneck, rooted in a capitalist psychology of scarcity and privilege.

"We adjust our methods," said Fidel, "to what is possible, and to our economic and social objectives. We are not like a capitalist; we do not have limitations set by a market. Here we are not going to pay someone 370 dollars to eliminate a cow as they do in Europe — while at the same time consumption of milk in Europe is less than a litre *per capita* — simply because of the problem of a market for milk. We believe that human beings need far more than a litre *per capita* . . . and our limits are set not by a market but by need. Our limit is optimum consumption" (May 17, 1969).

On this reasoning he had geared the cattle industry, a potential money spinner, to the financially unrewarding business of providing fresh milk for everybody. "In cattle-raising we have given first priority to milk as this is the most complete food, one which is especially necessary for children, elderly people, the sick and others."

But, Preston argued, why not produce meat for use, sell the surplus for vital foreign exchange, and import milk? After all Cubans needed meat as well as milk. They were hungry and hard up and raising beef cattle would be both quicker and cheaper. Castro's answer in effect was "fresh milk is essential not only for Cuba, but for the third world, with whom we identify, and which now spends millions importing milk or does without it. Our experience in milk-production will be invaluable to that world. Many countries in the third world already export meat to the developed countries — the tragic colonial pattern of the starving feeding the well-fed. Cuba will help break that pattern. And apart from everything else it will be an exciting creative challenge. Meat will be produced once our dairy-herds are stabilized by crossing the Zebu bull with Holstein cows, producing beef cattle that weigh 1,200 pounds at twelve months."

The question was crucial because, as Preston saw it, Cuban conditions were far less suitable for milk-production than for meat, and Cubans might end up with neither meat nor milk. There was no dairy experience, no tradition, and dairy cows needed the kind of attention that underdeveloped people were incapable of giving them. Equally important was the question of cattle feed. Enough milk couldn't be produced from Cuban pastures, so the cows ought to be raised in barns and fattened on corn.

Here again Fidel disagreed and advocated pasture. "We don't import feed for milk production," he told Camaguey farmers (*Granma*, September 25, 1966). "We believe that herbage is the most economic fodder for cattle, and especially pangola. If aside from pangola we give the cattle leguminous plants which are four times richer in calcium than gramineous plants, and contain twice as much protein, we would have the ideal pasturage. The best legume for our purposes is kudsu, which so far is the one that has adapted the best to our soil and climate. Alfalfa is magnificent, but we are still working on varieties suitable for our country."

In their book *Soviet Communism and Agrarian Revolution*, Roy and Betty Laird wrote: "The most gloomy of the lingering shadows on [Soviet] agricultural science is an indication that the leadership still tends to pass judgments in the technical realm. Perhaps Khrushchev's greatest mistake in agricultural affairs was his repeated insistence upon telling the farms in one area to grow corn, and those in another to grow peas, or to argue that science supported a particular type of cultivation. In total, such actions merit the subsequent charges of 'subjectivity', and the revival of the 'cult of the personality'. Perhaps, however, his acts were more a reflection of an inescapable weakness in the Soviet leadership system than an expression of his particular personality. Whatever the cause of Khrushchev's intervention in realms beyond his competence, however, the point is that even if agricultural scientists must be expected to err occasionally in their technical judgments, on such matters a wise leadership must accept the fact that the agricultural specialists will be more often right than the leaders. Moreover, if enthusiastic contributions from the scientists is to be encouraged, their judgment must be accepted in technical matters unless overriding political or economic considerations clearly call for an alternative course of action."

Doctor Preston felt that Fidel was an amateur geneticist getting kicks from a multi-million-dollar experiment. He was angered by Castro's habit of arguing, when it suited him, by assertion, by halftruth, by deliberately missing the point and by pounding away at irrelevancies. Also by his ignorance. "Castro," he told me, "goes round saying that the F.1 inherits milk characteristics from the Holstein and strength from the Zebu, and they all repeat it, and it is nonsense." I remarked that Fidel, in full knowledge of Dr Preston's hostility, had made several grateful references to his achievements in Cuba; that whatever Fidel's mistakes, the revolution had succeeded because of a succession of crucially wise decisions, and that in spite of years of bitter disagreement, Fidel hadn't sacked him. His views were aired, his research was published and praised. Not only did Fidel have the vision and seriousness to push through with scientific farming on a large scale, but he hired experts who were free to tell their Cuban students and everybody else that Fidel was a fool. Why not bury the hatchet? It might help Cuba. Doctor Preston answered that all he wanted was to be left alone to do his research.

Doctor Malcolm Willis gave me as an example of Fidel's ignorance, "the recent gandul fiasco". Fidel had been looking for suitable legumes to supplement pangola, so "somebody did a few experiments in a pot and came up with gandul as an answer to the problem. Castro announced it, *Granma* duly echoed him, thousands of people poured out to plant gandul. It turned out that cattle don't even eat gandul, and when they did it tended to make them sick. Anybody who read the literature would know that. The Americans and Indians both rejected it years ago. And Cuban *campesinos* traditionally planted gandul hedges because they kept off cattle. Fidel needed a magic feed, so some little Lysenko came up with this one. The programme folded."

I checked this story with some of the people involved, and it was true. One man said he knew gandul didn't work, but if he'd said so he would be out on a limb. Another said he'd refused to plant it in his province. "But," he added, "in Cuba, no matter what our mistakes, Cubans have the last word. Anyway the gandul wasn't a total failure because people can eat the beans, though often we just didn't have enough labour to harvest them."

The low level of research that the gandul fiasco indicated, made Preston and Willis contemptuous of most of their Cuban colleagues. Fidel complained that "certain problems of treatment, certain lack of knowledge, certain inconsiderations, brought about hurt feelings on the part of comrades from other organizations. They felt hurt, they felt mistreated, and some of their work was even rejected. They felt themselves to be the victims of a certain contempt" (May 17, 1969).

Preston and Willis would not, of course, have been contemptuous of mere ignorance, which they expected, and which they were employed to correct, but they hated the combination of ignorance with a stubborn determination to have the last word. They ignored the fact that the mainspring of the revolution was revolt against foreign assumptions of superiority. Cubans were fed to the teeth with tutelage and would rather make mistakes than persist in a psychology of dependence. This Preston and Willis tended to regard as political rubbish which interfered with science and bred charlatans like Castro.

"They have the confidence of the people," Doctor Willis told me, "and they abuse it." Cuba, he said with utter exasperation, could be the perfect place for agricultural development. Scientific policies could be carried out across the board. No private interests

or stubborn ancient customs to interfere. But instead politics interfered; Fidel was a politician dabbling in science. This was fatal.
Politics and science didn't mix. "My students go to so many meetings I find them asleep in the library in the afternoon. They are
always going out to do voluntary labour. All it does is ruin their
boots, which are made of cardboard anyway. These political types
don't have the mental energy for really detailed effort. They go into
politics to get easy kudos and perks. They are the ones who are sent
abroad on conferences. They can't risk sending the bright people
out of the country. They won't come back. The dead-heads have
to come back because they would starve anywhere else. The keenest
party people are the worst."

Because of their contempt for Fidel's scientific conclusions,
Preston and Willis tended to reject his broad view that the Cuban
cattle industry should produce milk by grazing cows on cultivated
pasture. They stuck to their own view that what the country should
produce was beef cattle, fed on corn in barns; and according to
Fidel they did little research on milk-producing using pasture,
although this was the policy of the Government. "The Institute of
Animal Science," said Fidel, "should have carried out an intensive
profound study of pasturing methods, on the yield of our pastures,
on the yield in meat and above all in milk. As you may have noticed
milk has been practically ignored in the research programme of the
Institute. I am only telling the truth. Go over the entire programme,
examine all the work, and you will find that meat was given much
more attention on the strength of hypothetical meat exports, at a
time when we had not solved our country's milk requirements,
inasmuch as if we are to supply our people with one quart of milk a
day *per capita*, we must produce some eight million quarts of milk
every day. And the problem of milk had to be studied. But milk, like
pastures, was given a minimum of attention by the Institute of
Animal Science" (May 17, 1969).

Fidel felt that there was little to recommend Preston's policy of
feeding grain in barns. "I believe it will be a long time, very long,
before it will be worthwhile keeping our herds in barns and having

to employ thousands upon thousands of pieces of machinery in order to carry feed to them. Pasture offers us the excellent opportunity of cattle working for us instead of us working for cattle." He also rejected corn as a European solution. It was his "firm opinion" that cultivated pasture would produce three times as much beef yield as any of the varieties of corn grown in Cuba, and Preston had produced no research to disprove this. And pastures were perennial whereas corn had to be planted every year — a process made excessively difficult by the Cuban climate.

"Ours was never a cereal-grain-producing or a soybean-producing country. Two problems exist; the lack of a tradition in the cultivation of these crops and the unfavourable climatic conditions for them. The unfavourable climate conditions consist of the fact that in our country there are certain long periods of drought and the fact that the rainy season begins abruptly.

"This is not the case in many countries with a temperate climate where the soil is prepared before winter comes and where part of it is even planted before the winter sets in; where, as soon as the snow melts, the moisture necessary for planting vast areas to grain is found in the already ploughed and prepared soil. In our country we have to prepare the soil and then wait for the first shower, and when it comes it is sometimes followed by the regular rains. So, long before these areas can be planted, the weeds have already come up.

"Moreover, without irrigation in our agriculture, we would be forced to employ a huge number of machines [and risk them sinking in mud].

"The experience of planting more than 1,200,000 acres to sugarcane for the 1970 harvest in fifteen months has clearly demonstrated how hard it is to carry out such a task, and how it was necessary, in many cases, to prepare and plant the land using ox-drawn instead of motorized equipment.

"Problems such as plagues and disease in a climate such as ours are well known; the scrub and the struggle against scrub and plagues in a climate such as ours are well known . . . It is true that, with corn, as with many other plants, many adaptations have been achieved which have made it possible through selection and through genetics to develop strains resistant to climatic conditions which were not the conditions found in the places where those plants originated. But it was necessary to develop and test these new strains exhaustively before plunging along that road; we needed to know how we were going to tackle the problem of planting all that land to corn at the beginning of spring; how we were going to do this job in those broad areas of the country which did not have adequate drainage; how we were going to solve the problem of securing adequate lands when a large part of the best lands were already planted to sugar-cane; and how we were going to solve the problem of hurricanes.

"Why should our country be involved in a type of agriculture that makes it necessary to plough an enormous land area every year in order to plant corn? Why should our country adapt itself to an animal nutrition system which is perfectly justified in temperate climates in Europe, and in most of the United States, where the winters are long, where they can plough large areas of land and where they are even forced to do it so as to achieve the maximum utilization of the land in a short period of time? Looking at it the other way around, why should we give up the excellent advantages of a climate such as that of this country? Why should we give up the advantages of the absence of cold winters, the absence of snow and the possibility of the all-year-round growing of perennial plants — which do not oblige us to plough the land every year? Why not avail ourselves of the advantages of pastures growing under the conditions of our climate?

"There was absolutely no comparison. There are types of cultivated pastures which can be kept up indefinitely and whose yield can even be increased every year; which are drought-resistant; which bounce back at the first rain; and which, when irrigated and fertilized adequately, can maintain uniform production almost all year around.

"If, in addition to this, we had the possibility, with our limited stock of machines, earmarked for other crops (mainly sugar-cane), for the direct production of other food staples — if we had the possibility to develop cattle on a really economical basis, why should we plunge into a much more costly system which requires a greater amount of resources and which, due to our country's conditions, is less safe?

"Thus, two opinions were counterposed: the opinion that the solution was to be found in the use of grain, and the opinion that the solution was to be found in the use of pastures. So, a kind of ideological controversy arose in the field of science — if you agree to call it science — or, if you prefer, you may call it the field of practice or the field of reality. Nevertheless, we did not pressure, we did not impede the development of their research and the tests to find solutions through the use of grains. By requesting and insisting, we succeeded in having some research done on pastures, a limited number of research projects.

"We read the work presented here by engineer Quintana on research on beef production through the use of pastures, the test with napier, the growing of napier and alfalfa, the growing of guinea grass with kudsu. We remember very well how we succeeded in having this research carried out.

"There was some resistance on the part of the Institute to doing this research work, and we had to secure a number of acres of land and ask some Cuban comrades to go ahead and conduct the research.

"A curious thing happened, however. The main objective of that research was to find out how much beef could be produced on one acre of land through the use of pastures. And it was our firm opinion that, given the conditions of our climate, the yield of one acre of some forage plants, with adequate fertilization and irrigation, would be three times that of an acre planted to corn.

"To our great surprise, we saw that the objective of the research was hardly mentioned at all and that the conclusion of how much beef can be produced on one acre was never arrived at: instead, this work consisted practically of a comparative test of various breeds and their response to forage. It was certainly a surprise for us to see that a test whose object was to ascertain the superiority of pasture over grain should in the end become a test to find out what the response of the various breeds to pasture feeding would be. The main objective had been practically sidetracked and forgotten" (May 17, 1969).

It is possible that Doctor Preston underrated the traumatic effect of the battle against disease, drought, flood and weeds that Cubans have had to face for ten years in planting and harvesting cane. A heavy planting programme such as a venture into corn is clearly not something they would want to risk if there is a chance that pasture would prove the better solution. But to Doctor Preston, Fidel sounded like Khrushchev, who also set up as an expert and turned forty million hectares of land into a dustbowl.

As it turned out Preston did some brilliant research on molasses which introduced an alternative to grain. He suggested that Fidel raise cattle in barns and feed them mainly molasses, which Cuba produces in vast quantities. Fidel praised the work on molasses, but argued that it would have to remain a supplement to the main diet of pasture. He argued that by 1980 Cuba will have "many more than fifteen million head of cattle", plus millions of hogs and poultry. All these would be fed molasses, and even if Cubans planted twice as much cane as they now plant, and turned half of it into molasses there "simply wouldn't be enough". Of course it would be feasible in Cuba to plant three times as much cane and use most of it for molasses, but molasses fetches a high price on the world market and it might be more economical to use it as a supplementary diet.

The whole argument between Fidel and his British advisers came to a head at the Congress of the Institute of Animal Science in May 1969, attended by eminent scientists from all over the world. Doctor Preston planted the fuse in his opening speech.

"My task tonight is to say something about the organization of this congress. I believe that at least some of you already know something about its organization. Undoubtedly some of you know that this congress has a scientific level. It probably does not have the highest level in the world, but, undoubtedly, some of you know that it has a certain level.

"I remember the first congress I attended [in Cuba], at the Capitol building in 1965. I do not need to mention the agency which organized that congress, but I remember a session in which the chairman was reading a newspaper. In short, this can give some indication. If the chairman was more interested in the newspaper than in the lecture of the speaker, it indicates that that congress did not have a very high scientific level.

"One thing I am sure of: in this congress our chairmen will never be found reading newspapers . . .

"One original objective of this congress was to set up a forum, a time and place in which Cuban researchers could meet to discuss research work, to present papers and to have them published, because you can never have research without its being published.

"Another objective of a congress of this nature is teaching, to teach young research workers. Why? Because the congress is taking place in Cuba now. But any scientist who is going to reach a level someday will leave the country to represent it at an international congress. And that is why it is very important for these Cuban scientists to know how to behave at an international congress.

"It is logical, for example, not to send a sports delegation, a baseball team, to an international event abroad without giving this team, this group of young people, very good training. This is something that is done quite well in Cuba. The same thing applies to science: you cannot leave a country to participate in an international congress without every research worker being well trained in how to conduct himself at an international congress. This is an important objective.

"Last night Professor Cooper, who is with us, told me that in some international organizations there are two types of selection of papers. There is one type which they have for scientists from developed countries — a very high standard — and there is a second type of selection which they have for developing countries.

"I want to tell Professor Cooper and any of the other guest

scientists here who in the future will take part in congresses abroad
that whenever they receive the papers of our Institute to apply the
judgment of the first group, of the developed countries. It is a fact
that this country is in the process of development from an economic
point of view. We accept this. But we will never accept the idea
that there can be underdevelopment in the selection of scientific
work . . .

"I also want to say this for the benefit of the young people among
you, the young researchers who are the future of the country: if you
want to follow the line of a scientist, you must always struggle. You
must struggle against tradition, you must always struggle against
bureaucracy. That is the way we struggled in England, and we
continue to struggle in Cuba.

"Young research workers, you must believe and understand that
science must win."

Fidel answered: "Why say that here in the first congress to be
held in this country — as though we were some sort of Siboney
Indians, or something like that, some backward people — that in
the first scientific congress in this country, the chairman of the
session, who was precisely the President of the Academy of Sciences,
was reading a newspaper? So imagine what sort of a congress that
was, in which the chairman of the institution was reading a newspaper! What need is there for such insults, for such affronts? And
on top of that we are told that Cubans are going to learn how to
behave at an international congress, that we are going to learn how
to behave when we go abroad. We Cubans will certainly be starting
off on the right foot if we learn to behave like this in an international
congress, beginning by offending the country in which the congress
is taking place, offending those present at the congress! Strange
things are occurring at this congress, at this historic congress!"

Fidel then gave his version of his relations with Doctors Preston
and Willis. "We know that certain specialists, including Doctor
Willis, have bestowed on me the title of director of genetics in Cuba,
commenting that where have they ever seen a Prime Minister
concerned with such things, and that I know nothing about the

matter, which may be true to some extent, and I don't deny it. But I am guided by an interest, and that is the interest of the people! And I certainly do not believe that it is a mistake or a crime that among the responsibilities to the people I include concern for these questions, if I try to study them, if I try to understand them — if only slightly — and if I try to find solutions. And this is a painful necessity in our country, where there are not many scientists, where there are not many specialists and where those of us who must assume the responsibility for finding solutions to these problems do not even get the correct advice for finding these solutions . . . We do not pretend to be scientists. That would be absurd. Unfortunately the countless obligations which we have in many matters would prevent us from ever devoting ourselves to that hypothetical aspiration. We aspire to at least a minimum knowledge so as to be able to evaluate the advice that can be given . . . And the road our nation has followed is to produce cross-breeds of potential dairy-herds known as F.1s, cross-breeds which displease Doctor Willis and Doctor Preston."

To prove their displeasure with the F.1s, Preston, Willis and a Cuban scientist called Clark produced a piece of research that rocked the conference. The paper, presented by Clark, challenged Fidel's statistics about the milk capacity of the F.1.

According to Fidel's figures some F.1s, under favourable conditions, produced as much as thirty litres a day, and the average yield on scores of farms all over the country was "up to nine litres using pastures without concentrates" (1 litre = 1·1 quarts). But the paper presented by Preston, Willis and Clark claimed that in fact the F.1 produced as little milk as the Zebu. On their research fifteen F.1s produced an average of 370 litres in seventy-two days — just over five litres a day, and eighty per cent of them were dry at one hundred days. In another experiment where thirty F.1s were handled differently (after calving they were milked manually for a period of seven days in the presence of the calf, but without letting the calf suck) they averaged only five hundred and sixty-one litres in one hundred and thirty-three days, and fifty-three per cent were dry at

one hundred days. In a third experiment with a group of fifteen
F.1s handled like the second group twenty-six point six per cent
were dry at one hundred days.

The experiments also showed that under Cuban conditions pure-
bred Holsteins averaged eight litres, and a milking period of two
hundred and fifty days. These results, though described as "tentative", underlined the Preston thesis that meat ought to be produced,
not milk, and implied that Castro's dairy cattle policy pursued at
enormous expense and against expert advice was a failure. Castro
was raising bad cows on expensive land. It also implied that the
claims of the various genetic centres about their F.1s were not
scientific, and that there was a Lysenko squint.

Fidel hit the roof: "Now then — and this is really amazing! — a
work has been presented here . . . even if it was called 'tentative' . . .
I would not dare to present anything tentative on something about
which I did not have the minimum of knowledge necessary to
establish its validity. This is not a question just of presenting works
for the sake of presenting something. Now then, can such a thesis
stand? No, it cannot. Can this be investigated and verified? Yes,
it can: the nature of the paper, the error such a paper entails, the
low quality and the superficiality of the research, the disorientation
this paper entails for all the cattle raisers in this country and for
others who work with our cattle — and there are already half a
million F.1s! Does this mean perhaps that we are not happy
because research was done which yielded adverse results? No . . .
We do not hold dogmatic opinions on any of these questions. But we
do believe that since comrades who work in cattle-raising are
present, we cannot allow them to leave quietly under the impression
they have worked in vain. If this were true we would say we have
worked in vain, but let us begin anew. But this is not so. And there
are many comrades here — we have the results of genetic centres —
but it seems that the results of scores of F.1 farms are similar:
average yields of up to nine litres, using pastures, without
concentrates."

Yet it disturbed him that none of these comrades had got up and said this. "Faced by the data given here in the paper — what a phenomenon: nobody, with the exception of Comrade Teresa Planas of the National Office of Genetics thought of asking whether it was true or not ... Frankly speaking I was saddened by the fact ... "

He then produced proof of *his* claims. "I am not asking [visiting scientists] to believe what I say. I can ask this of Cubans, of course, because they know that we don't fool around with lies or demaguery. As far as the [foreign] technicians are concerned we have no right but to submit the facts to the test. I believe this is very important, because Latin America has tens of millions of herds of cattle of this type. Other countries have hundreds of millions ... There is a group of cows here on which we have quite a lot of information because they are the results of the first crossings made. We have witnessed the entire development of this programme, we are quite familiar with it, because it was precisely these results which helped us find the solution to the milk problem. This is a lot of forty-five F.1 cows. They are at Bijiritas. Here are their names and their numbers. All these cows exist in reality, they are producing milk now — and those who have any doubts can go there and verify how the measurements were made, how these results were obtained, what they are based on. All those cows and all those centres are at the disposal of all the investigators who visit our country. (A) thirty-seven — ten of them still in production — reached 244 milking days, which represents 82·2 per cent of the total number of cows. (B) twenty — seven of them still in production — reached 305 milking days, which represents 44·4 per cent of the total numbers. (C) Their average age at calving was twenty-eight months, thus they were in calf at an average age of nineteen months. We must point out that the average calving age ranges from twenty-five to thirty-four months. (D) The average of total milking days — including those that went dry prematurely — was two hundred and eighty-four days. It must be remembered that we intentionally cause the cows to go dry after seven months gestation. (E) The production averages reached are, for forty-five cows in total milking, 11·8 litres a day; for thirty-seven cows in 244 days milking, 13 litres a day; and for twenty cows in 305 days milking, 13·1 litres a day.

"In the first milking period only seven out of forty-five cows produced less than 2,000 litres. The average at the Institute of Animal Science was 370 litres while here only seven produced less than 2,000.

"Thirty-eight out of forty-five — 84 per cent — produced over 2,000 litres; twenty-five out of forty-five — over 55 per cent — produced over 3,000 litres; sixteen out of forty-five — 35 per cent — produced over 4,000 litres, and eight out of forty-five — 17 per cent — produced over 5,000 litres. In other words eight out of forty-five went over 5,000 litres, while only seven went below 2,000 litres. Three out of forty-five went over 6,000 litres, and one, which is still producing milk — is getting close to the 7,000 litre mark.

"What happened in the second milking? ... " And here Fidel produced a second set of figures, no less detailed ... "I would estimate that this herd of cows will average from 4,000–4,500 litres of milk during the milking period. So by eliminating one out of ten — and in any herd with an average production of over fifteen litres a selection is always made — by eliminating one out of every ten we can get average yields of milk almost equal to the Netherlands, a country with a temperate climate and traditionally a dairy nation. The F.1, the crossing of the Zebu and Holstein, in the second milking, can reach a tested average of from 4,000–4,500 litres, eliminating one out of ten cows, with a fat content of not less than four per cent ... These are things that can be verified by all the participants in this Congress.

"Then what factor can have led to the presentation of such a paper? Certainly I do not believe this could have been done deliberately, that this could have been a dishonest thing. What can have led the Institute of Animal Science to have come up with a misleading, false and confusing thing of that nature? Simple subjectivity, and it has led to more than one mistake in research work as a result of dealing with problems in a superficial and negligent manner."

I asked Doctor Lawrence Synge, 1955 Nobel Prize winner in chemistry, who has no special knowledge in Preston's field but who attended the conference, what the general reaction was to the Preston/Willis/Clark paper, and he told me that people said the cows in Preston's experiment hadn't been milked on Christmas Day. Doctor Willis had in fact told me this in January, giving it as an example of the kind of attention dairy-cows were likely to get in Cuba. The Christmas Day figures would make a litre or so difference to the daily average but they make no difference to the length of the milking period which is an equally crucial factor.

The question put to Clark by Teresa Planas of the National Office of Genetics seems to me relevant: "I would like to ask the comrade a personal question: in his opinion does the data given here represent the performances of the F.1 on a national scale?"

Clark replied that the "cows tested are not representative of the F.1 population of our country because of ... the problem of handling." If this is not merely equivocation it suggests that the cows in the Preston experiment were handled less successfully than the cows on farms all over the country. Perhaps Preston's tentative results will, as Clark suggested, be corrected by further research — research that will have to be done by others, since Preston and Willis have now left Cuba.

Fidel and
the United States

The central issue in the cattle quarrel was the basic belief of Preston and Willis that dairy cows need the kind of attention that Cubans are unlikely to give them, therefore it is more sensible to raise beef cattle — especially as they themselves were specialists in the production of beef. Fidel on the other hand would see to it that if he had the right cows and the right feed, the cows would get adequate attention, particularly on the state farms, so he could go ahead with a cattle industry that produced both meat and milk, and save the country millions of dollars that would otherwise have to be used to import milk and milk products such as cheese and ice-cream.

"If we had asked the Institute of Animal Science how we would solve the problem of milk there would still be no answer but that the F.1 goes dry after seventy-two days, and produces 370 litres of milk, exactly the same as the Zebu cow. That is, the moral would be: give up all hope of having milk in this country for many years" (May 17, 1969).

Fidel's view of the competence, and therefore, ultimately, of the living standards, of Cuba and the third world has again and again turned out to be different from that of foreign experts. There is an unconscious double-standard assumed even by liberals. While striving for better conditions in the third world, they take for granted that these will fall short of complete equality with the developed world. At the beginning of the revolution Fidel had to reject the view of friendly foreign experts that countries like Cuba with unemployment problems should use more manual labour and less machinery. This perfectly logical economic view ignores the effect of men having to work like mules under a tropical sun. It also takes for granted a much slower rate of development than was in fact achieved in Cuba. Had Fidel adopted it he wouldn't have sent most of his unemployed young people to school, Cuba's extraordinary educational programme wouldn't have been possible, and without this programme the present swift technological development would have taken decades or been completely lost in the quicksands of gradualism. He would have pushed for far less Russian aid than he was in fact able to get and use. He would have betrayed a colonized vision.

It was, above all, his rejection of the US military double-standard in the hemisphere, which takes for granted Latin American weakness and North American strength, that made him create an army which could beat off the Giron (Bay of Pigs) invasion, and saved the revolution. Arthur Schlesinger's account of Giron shows how Latin American military weakness was abused even by Kennedy. During the Kennedy administration Cuban exiles, trained by the CIA in Guatemala, attacked Cuba, killing and wounding hundreds of Cubans in an attempt to destroy the revolution. Thousands more would have been killed if the expected civil war had ensued. Schlesinger had advised Kennedy that the invasion, originally planned by President Eisenhower, "would dissipate all the extraordinary goodwill which has been rising towards the new administration through the world. It would fix a malevolent image of the new administration in the mind of millions" (*A Thousand Days*). Kennedy himself was decidedly ambivalent. Why then did the invasion take place? Schlesinger's explanation, while I believe it, is unbelievable.

"The determination to keep the scheme alive sprang in part, I believe, from the embarrassments of calling it off. As Dulles [Allen Dulles, brother of John Foster and head of the CIA] said at the March 11th meeting, 'Don't forget that we have a disposal problem. If we take these men out of Guatemala we will have to transfer them to the United States, and we can't have them wandering around the country telling everyone what they have been doing.' What could one do with 'this asset' if not send it on to Cuba? If transfer to the United States was out, demobilization on the spot would create even greater difficulties. The Cubans themselves were determined to go back to their homeland, and they might well forcibly resist efforts to take away their arms and equipment. Moreover even if the brigade was disbanded, its members would disperse, disappointed and resentful, all over Latin America. They would tell where they had been, and what they had been doing, thereby exposing CIA operations. And they would explain how the United States, having prepared an expedition against Castro, lost its nerve. This could only result, Dulles kept emphasizing, in discrediting Washington, disheartening Latin American opponents of Castro, and encouraging the Fidelistas in their attacks on democratic regimes, like that of Betancourt in Venezuela. Disbandment might thus produce pro-Castro revolutions all around the Caribbean. For all these reasons, CIA argued, instead of turning the Cubans loose we should find some means for putting them back into Cuba 'on their own' ...

"Having created the Brigade as an option, the CIA now presented its use against Cuba as a necessity. Nor did Dulles's arguments lack force. Confronted by them Kennedy tentatively agreed that the simplest thing, after all, might be to let the Cubans go where they yearned to go — to Cuba. Then he tried to turn the meeting to a consideration of how this could be done with the least political risk" (*A Thousand Days*, page 219).

Faced with this standard imperialistic logic, and its acceptance by liberals as "not lacking force", the Cubans got hold of the same kind of offensive missiles that the United States possessed. The missiles, installed by the Russians, didn't affect the military balance between Russia and the United States, but did affect the military balance between Cuba and the United States. Cuba for the first time would no longer be totally at the mercy of liberal administrations. With the prevailing double-standard in the hemisphere, however, this new balance of power was so intolerable that Kennedy was willing to risk nuclear war. The *status quo* which ensures that 180 million North Americans can destroy 300 million Latin Americans without reprisal, was taken for granted by all Kennedy liberals, by all Latin American Uncle Toms, and even by friends of Castro like the decidedly anti-imperialistic Herbert Matthews, a distinguished journalist then working for the *New York Times*:

"The 'crisis of the Caribbean' as the Cubans call it, was a shocking experience for Castro, but I have a suspicion that he took a certain satisfaction and pride that he, Fidel Castro, a Cuban, could have brought the world to the brink of nuclear holocaust. I do not mean that he wanted or expected a nuclear war. He was thinking in terms of the defence of Cuba, and the defensive relationship of the 'socialist world' towards American 'imperialism'. Yet, it was within his power — one young Cuban's power — to permit Khrushchev to install the missiles, or to refuse to permit the Russians to do so. No Latin American ever had such power. Let us hope that none will ever have such power again." (*Castro: a Political Biography*.)

The rôle of the American liberal thus appears to be to applaud the imbalance of power, and to deplore each result of it. Cuba is invaded, the invasion is regretted as abuse of power; Santo Domingo is then duly invaded and duly lamented as power abused. Between the American right, centre and left there is the complete cycle of crime, restrained crime, and liberal repentance that makes US democracy unassailable.

The military double-standard in the hemisphere results, as one would expect, in an economic double-standard. In Kennedy-liberal eyes Puerto Rico, for example, is a success story, and Munoz Marin, its ex-governor, the kind of Latin American to support. In just under thirty years, from 1940, Munoz led his country to the stage where officially it has only fifteen per cent unemployed; where only one out of six Puerto Ricans in greater San Juan lives in slums — slums that smell of shit and let in the rain, and that will disappear at the present rate of slum-clearance in two hundred years; where

out of three and a half million Puerto Ricans, one million live in the
US, most of them in appalling conditions in New York city; where
those remaining at home have an average *per capita* income one
third as high as the poorest state in the US, a *per capita* average that
is moreover not a true average, and hides unbelievable inequality.
Worse conditions exist in Venezuela, rich in oil. One out of three
people in Caracas lives in a slum. Yet Schlesinger describes
Venezuela as "a model for progressive Latin American democracy", and praises Munoz Marin as "the remarkable Governor of
Puerto Rico". Similarly, at the beginning of the crisis in the
Dominican Republic he quotes President Kennedy as saying,
"There are three possibilities in descending order of preference: a
decent democratic regime, a continuation of the Trujillo regime, or
a Castro regime. We ought to aim at the first, but we really can't
renounce the second until we are sure that we can avoid the third."
(*A Thousand Days*.) On the same page Schlesinger points out that
"since 1930 Trujillo had operated a cruel and efficient dictatorship."
By efficient he means efficiently cruel, since living standards were
low even by Latin American standards.

In a power situation only a fool expects anything but a precarious
charity, and Cubans have given up this folly. They no longer expect
any change in US attitudes. Instead they summon Latin America
to bloody revolution under the flaming banner of Che.

"It is," said Che, "absolutely right to avoid all useless sacrifices.
Therefore it is so important to clear up the real possibilities that
dependent America may have of liberating itself through pacific
means. For us the solution to this question is quite clear: the present
moment may or may not be the proper one for starting the struggle,
but we cannot harbour any illusions, and we have no right to do so,
that freedom can be obtained without fighting. And these battles
shall not be mere street fights with stones against tear gas bombs,
or pacific general strikes; neither shall it be the battle of a furious
people destroying in two or three days the repressive scaffolds of
the ruling oligarchs; the struggle shall be long, harsh, and its front
shall be in the guerrilla's refuge, in the cities, in the homes of the

fighters — where the repressive forces shall go seeking easy victims among their families — in the massacred rural population, in the villages or cities destroyed by the bombardments of the enemy. They are pushing us into this struggle; there is no alternative: we must prepare it, and we must decide to undertake it.

"The beginnings will not be easy ... Our mission in the first hour will be to survive: later we shall follow the perennial example of the guerrilla, carrying out armed propaganda — in the Vietnamese sense, that is, the bullets of propaganda, of the battles won or lost, but fought, against the enemy. The great lesson of the invincibility of the guerrilla taking root in the dispossessed masses; the galvanizing of the national spirit; the preparation for harder tasks, for resisting even more violent repressions; hatred as an element of the struggle; a relentless hatred of the enemy, impelling us over and beyond the natural limitations that man is heir to and transforming him into an effective, violent, selective and cold killing machine. Our soldiers must be thus; a people without hatred cannot vanquish a brutal enemy ... Our every action is a battle cry against imperialism, and a battle hymn for the people's unity against the great enemy of mankind: the United States of America. Wherever death may surprise us, let it be welcome, if this our battle cry reach some receptive ear, and another hand seize and shoulder our weapons, and other men intone the funeral dirge with the staccato singing of machine-guns and new battle cries of war and victory."

Perhaps future Latin American revolutionaries will avoid the communist label, and display, or even feel, no hostility to the United States. In this way they might allay legitimate fears that revolution in Latin America would cut off vital sources of supplies from the United States, for motives including revenge and hatred of capitalism. This the United States must surely guard against. It could best do so by seeking the goodwill of those countries whose trade it needs, not their weakness and degradation. But this would mean resisting the temptations of power and cant, controlling monopolies, facing the US electorate with higher prices, competing with the communist bloc which has at least twice as high a growth rate, overcoming the nagging fear that so-called free societies are in the long run unable to match the terms of trade offered by so-called totalitarian societies to the underdeveloped countries. All this may prove too difficult. The present policies are more fatal but easier. Much simpler to shout communism and march into Vietnam, Cuba and Santo Domingo.

Liberals condemn such actions, but even to liberal American administrations Trujillo is preferable to Castro who has "brought communism into the hemisphere".

The liberal proposition is that Castro should face cold-war realities, make do with US aid, build up his economy more slowly — even discreetly nationalizing some US property if necessary, using the income to modernize the masses, educate technicians and introduce technology. This view accepts cold-war realities only to reject the realities of US capitalism. In the decade of the Alliance for Progress, the United States has not even been able to stabilize Latin American export prices. As *Granma* accurately pointed out "unequal trade conditions have produced an annual loss of a billion dollars; the foreign debt has risen to six billion dollars and inflation has reached catastrophic proportions." That was August 1966. Today things are worse and the only liberal answer is the false arithmetic of birth-control: GNP and growth rate are rising, so stop population growth and there is progress. But how do you stop population growth, how long does it take, what would be the economic effects to the US of the loss of cheap labour and cheap products? And as Cuban students constantly asked me, is the resulting El Dorado to be a society like the United States? On present showing the only hope for Latin America is to find markets outside the United States, which by US definition means bringing communism into the hemisphere, which means war.

In the meantime, under this shadow, Fidel struggles for independence both from the Soviet Union and the United States, providing Latin America with the example of a society that in a mere twelve years has shuffled off misery and chronic under-development.

On December 20, 1969, at the end of a decade, he talked to Cuban students about the past and future, soft-pedalling communism and its hostile cold-war implications, emphasizing socialism as a method of organization necessary for the third world, making clear that freedom can't be defined in terms of communism and anti-communism but as the capacity to make rational use of technology. His reflections are an expert summary of the revolutionary process and make an appropriate conclusion to this book.

"We mustn't forget that the [post-revolutionary] period of change in ownership and of change in the structure of property here led to anybody at all becoming a manager. There were times when even the village idiot was managing a sugar mill. Sometimes it was the greatest nitwit — my apologies to nitwits in general — who was doing the managing.

"It would be ridiculous to deny what happened when everybody became a farm administrator, an agricultural expert, with the change in agricultural structure, with the change in the structure of ownership, that we read about in text-books. Revolution is an easy word to say, but its depth in reality is something very serious.

"And when such a change takes place — not in the super-developed society that Marx foresaw, but in a super-underdeveloped society that nobody foresaw, a society made up of almost thirty per cent illiterates and ninety-five per cent of the rest semi-illiterates . . . After all, would anyone dare say that a man with only third-grade instruction was educated? What can a man with third-grade instruction do? Maybe he couldn't even get on the right bus to go home.

"All this in a society whose means of production were the ox, the hoe and the machete; in a country that imported everything and exported two or three products, principally sugar produced under technological conditions similar to those that prevailed four centuries ago. Four centuries ago — as today — sugar-cane was cut by hand, freed of its straw and thrown into a pile from which it was loaded into a cart and hauled to a mill.

"And it can be said truthfully that the economy of a country that depends on that method of production, with cane-cutting done by hand, is, as I told a group of comrades this morning, nothing but a 'rope-soled shoes' economy. It will provide for nothing better than rope-soled shoes. And the reason why all the people in this country did not go around wearing rope-soled shoes is because sixty per cent of them went around barefooted. Of course, there were some people who owned fifteen pairs of shoes while this was going on.

"So far as the countryside was concerned, shoes were a rarity. And the greater part of the population lived in rural areas.

"And an economy that depends on the productivity of men cutting sugar-cane by hand . . . And that was the productivity the country depended on, because what the country exported was mainly sugar. Everything else was 'wheeling and dealing'. Somebody sold something over here, somebody else traded something over there, and still somebody else exchanged things somewhere else, and so on. But the income, most of the gross national product, came from the cane.

"[The country had] 0·01 per cent technicians — and what technicians! — with a few honourable exceptions. Many of them were mediocre, with the mentality of lackeys of imperialism, easy to bribe, sell or buy, easily enrolled as spies . . . Suffice it to say that there were individuals here in charge of important jobs who had been CIA agents for the previous seven years, just to cite an example. This was possible because, besides being illiterate, we have been naïve. Naïve illiterates and semi-illiterates to the nth degree. And all these things have happened to us . . .

" . . . Far from being surprised at the enormous number of mistakes that have been committed, we should be surprised that the number was not even greater. Perhaps that is some consolation, because that's the way things were . . . And all these factors played their respective rôles: the idiot, the semi-illiterate and that other one all played their rôles . . .

" . . . Fortunately, we have created the conditions for having the most developed, most rational agriculture in the world. Did this happen because we became geniuses all of a sudden? Because we all became scientists all of a sudden? No! It happened simply because all of a sudden, we had created the conditions to make rational use and exploitation of the land. The minifundium is no longer acceptable as a method of land exploitation. It is an antiquated method. And the industrially developed world in Europe — which has more advanced technology, industry and machines at its disposal than we — is plagued by the minifundium system, a system which is irrational because it clashes with technology.

"A crop-dusting plane cannot operate in a region of minifundia. We have this problem right here, in Oriente Province. Whenever a herbicide-spraying plane skims over a large extent of cane-fields where there are seven miserable banana trees standing on a small plot of land nearby, three days later the banana trees are dead. It's really incredible, what a little herbicide blown by the wind can do.

"Modern technology — large combines, planes for spraying fertilizer over rice paddies, which makes it possible to increase the productivity in rice growing not a hundred times, but a thousand times — cannot be applied except within a system of agriculture that is physically rationalized, both in extent and in utilization. This is so, first of all, because modern technology and highly productive machines demand scope.

"Think of our rice-growing projects, where 90 hp tractors are being employed and where planes spreading herbicides or pesticides by means of a system of ultralow volume can produce fifteen times what planes using another system can produce: think of the levels of productivity we will obtain from these crops by utilizing large, standard machines and irrigation systems that may even be made to operate automatically. Someday our ricefields will consist of flat terraces, where the best advantage of the land has been taken, planted to the best and most highly productive strains, with irrigation through the use of automatic locks . . .

" ... The revolution has created conditions that permit making rational use of the land, both in extent and utilization; making farms of a size appropriate for the most modern techniques; and making the most efficient use of those farms, in keeping with the various crops being raised. This is the result of the conditions we have created, conditions which do not exist in developed Europe.

"In some highly developed countries it's a problem of land ownership. A man owns seven small farms of three and a half or four and a half acres each, and he has to use one machine to plough the land on all seven farms. Then come the all-purpose machines, and he is forced to do everything [with these] because otherwise he won't be able to take care of the farms. A man with eighteen acres cannot afford to have a tractor of X horsepower for ploughing and another tractor for another type of work.

"Fortunately, our country has created the social and political conditions to be able to apply technology without any limitations of any sort. This is why, in spite of the fact that we were illiterate — and, to a large extent, still are illiterate — the conditions exist, and technology is beginning to be applied ... In our country there used to be practically only one type of sugar-cane. We are testing and increasing our supply.

" ... We consider sugar-cane to be one of the most privileged plants in nature, the one with the greatest capacity for assimilating solar energy and turning it into carbohydrates. And carbohydrates, as you know, when submitted to fermentative processes, are a source of proteins. Moreover, sugar-cane has molasses; it has *bagasse*; it has leaves. *Bagasse* can be used in many ways — most important, it can be turned into protein. The leaves, too. And our country can have tens of millions of tons of those proteins, which can be turned into milk, meat, eggs and many other things.

"Hog-feeding presents a problem in our country now, due to the fact that corn is hard to grow in our climate — and, besides, an acre of corn cannot be compared in any way with an acre planted to cane. Given these circumstances, and as a by-product of the ten-million-ton harvest, we could, in the next few years, increase our

hog-breeding tremendously. As you know, unlike cattle, hogs repro-
duce very quickly. In a few years we could have any number of
them we wanted. Feed is the crux of the matter, and enriched
molasses and torula yeast are ideal for raising all the hogs we want in
our country.

"A program is already in preparation. Several hundred high-
quality hogs are being imported for an accelerated program to
develop our hog industry. And all of this is a product of our
cane.

"In this way, we can obtain from cane not only sugar and the
molasses used for different purposes, but also a source of proteins
and carbohydrates far superior to even the best corn or soybeans.

"Our climatic conditions have made this plant available to us, but
it has been the revolution that has created the conditions that allow
us to make extensive use of it — and we are going to do just that.

"Nevertheless, by 1980, sugar will account for considerably less
than thirty per cent of the gross national product of our agriculture.
(We exclude from this figure cane dedicated to other uses.) Those
who go around talking of monoculture are simply spouting nonsense, because this country has never before undertaken agricultural
diversification on such a scale as it is doing now.

"You all know that, in the past, whenever anyone here spoke of
producing rice, the sugar-mill owners scurried forth to proclaim
that, since our rice was bought from the United States, its production here would provoke reprisals against our sugar. As a result, rice
production was impossible, and everything was paralysed.

"In the past, our productive forces were delimited and held back
by social conditions. Today, this is no longer the case. For us, every
door is open for the development of the imagination, for the development of initiative, for the development of creativity and for economic
development in every field. Today, social conditions no longer hold
back our productive forces. Only ourselves, our own ignorance, can
hold us back now!

"Gentlemen, we ourselves constitute the principal obstacle today
to the development of our productive forces. The social and political

conditions have already been created for us to achieve their unlimited development. This is true.

"This is why I have gone into this brief and somewhat philosophic disquisition concerning the country that no one foresaw at the time of the advent of socialism.

"Because the first, brilliant conception of socialism was of socialism as a consequence of development.

"Marx conceived of socialism as the result of development. Today for the underdeveloped world, socialism is a necessary condition for development because without employing the socialist method — placing all the natural and human resources of the country at the service of the country, channelling these resources in the direction necessary to achieve the desired social objectives — no underdeveloped country can pull itself out of underdevelopment. You may be sure it can't.

"There can be as many political disquisitions as you like, as many doctrinaire discussions as you like, but we know from our own experience — lived here! — how difficult it is, even with every desire to carry it through, with nothing to stop us and with all of the revolutionary laws needed to do it — we know that there will be no economic development in any underdeveloped country without socialism, without centralizing all of the resources of the economy and channelling them in the needed direction.

"That is a fact. We have no need to preach. Why should we? We are neither campaigning nor propagandizing. When all is said and done let each one do whatever he can or whatever he chooses to.

"I am insisting on this point so that no one will think I am trying to offer advice to anyone. No one enjoys being given advice, and we don't enjoy giving it.

"I make this clarification for that reason, and I say this with complete conviction — conviction based on our experience: there will not be any development in any underdeveloped country in the world without socialism.

"When England, France and Germany were becoming developed, the situation was different. There were no developed countries in the world. None. And where there are no trees it is easy for a plant to grow. But, under a thick stand of forest, no plant can develop. And that is the situation for the underdeveloped countries: competition, subsidized production and the very often one-sided trade conditions that are imposed by the developed world with its unfair advantages and privileges and its developed technology while the countries of the underdeveloped world have neither technicians, research centres nor anything else. Not even a literate population, in a great many cases.

"Thus, while there are countries such as the United States which are now landing men on the moon with television coverage and all, in the underdeveloped world there are men who travel on donkeys and work with hoes, trying to produce enough food to survive.

"That is the comparative picture. The countries which developed their technology have moved farther and farther ahead. What does the future hold for the countries which do not attain development? What will be the future of the countries that do not develop? . . .

" . . . How can we bridge the enormous gap that separates the underdeveloped countries from those that have shot ahead? How can a country reduce the gap unless it be by taking advantage in a rational manner of even its least important economic resources, both natural and human? And how can this be achieved while these underdeveloped countries still indulge in the luxury of maintaining a high-living bourgeoisie that spends eighty per cent of the national income on conspicuous consumption while protesting against the one-sided trade conditions and the fact that very little is left to the underdeveloped! If any countries cannot afford that luxury, it is the underdeveloped ones! And this reality can be seen everywhere. This is the image of the underdeveloped world.

"And if there is no revolution, if socialist methods are not applied to develop the economy, there will not be the remotest hope of development, because, even with socialism, it's a difficult task. With socialism, revolution, and all, it's difficult; no one should underestimate it.

"All of this is with reference to sugar-cane and mechanization.

"Are there any more questions, or may I go now?"

ERNESTO ALVAREZ: Major, in addition to the agricultural and cattle-raising development to which our country will be committed, what other major lines of development are in view for the next five years?

FIDEL CASTRO: For the past few months, intensive work has been under way in framing a long-range development plan for 1970-80. Under our conditions, the question of a long-range plan isn't easy, because there are so many imponderable factors. And these imponderable factors are mainly related to one question: on what financial resources will we be able to count?

"Our country's credit has increased extraordinarily in the last few years. We now have possibilities for the acquisition of factories and equipment we couldn't even have dreamed of five or six years ago. Suffice it to say that in the years 1964-65, or even before that, in 1963, just getting a truck or a bulldozer — to say nothing of a fertilizer plant such as the one in Cienfuegos — was a difficult task, very problematic.

"So some factors of development depend entirely on us, while others depend on external resources. The external resources, in turn, depend on a series of circumstances, among them this country's seriousness in meeting its obligations; new international political circumstances; the consolidation of the revolution and its agricultural plans despite all adverse prognostications: the increasing discredit of the imperialist blockade, which constituted a serious obstacle to our country's possibilities of obtaining resources for its development.

"But we can now describe as a definite trend the incredible growth of our country's credit and prestige abroad and the trade offers made to Cuba from all over the world. In fact, large and important industrial sectors in the Western world that did not even bother to speak to us five years ago now take a very different attitude, and a series of contracts and negotiations have been developing with the rest of the world.

"We have a source of supply from abroad which is the socialist camp, principally the Soviet Union. Our large power plants, machine-building plants — such as the one in Santa Clara — machinery for the Antiliana de Acero Steel Plant, the important fertilizer complex in Nuevitas, the Fishing Port of Havana and other industrial installations have come from the Soviet Union . . .

" . . . But the truth is that we have a number of industrial needs, particularly those related to the development of our agriculture, as well as certain fields of industry, which must be met with equipment from nonsocialist areas, because, for technological reasons, no country in the world produces everything. We need certain equipment which is not available from the socialist camp.

"That is why I was saying that there are a number of imponderable factors that may contribute to more or less accelerated development in the next ten years. That is, in a country that is completely dependent upon importations, that must import ninety-five per cent of what it needs, there are certain factors which are beyond its control. It is not the case of a country that already has a number of basic installations. Our country doesn't even produce steel, with the single exception of the Antiliana de Acero plant — which is turning out a certain amount of steel rods — and a number of electric furnaces. Our country has no basic industries that would permit the drawing up of a program based mainly on our own resources. Therefore, our development programs will be, to a considerable degree, dependent on external factors.

"Now then, in the field of agriculture alone, we need a large number of plants to meet the country's consumer needs, on the one hand, and to produce exportable surpluses, on the other.

"You heard what I said with regard to the rice-drying plants needed for solving the problem of our rice supply, since the country can produce all the rice it needs as a result of the projects. But we need an incredible number of rice-drying plants. And we also need a large number of mills to process all of the rice needed by our people.

"In the coming years, especially until 1975, the dairy industry will require a considerable amount of expansion to satisfy the country's internal needs. Huge dairy herds are being built up, but the country's pasteurization installations, not to mention the technological state of many of them, are completely inadequate to meet consumers' needs for hygienic, fresh milk. Because we want to drink milk — not bacteria. And I can assure you that the people of this country have drunk considerably more bacteria than milk throughout their history. Of this I can assure you, because, in the greater part of the country, as in many places even today, milk was never pasteurized or refrigerated, and passed through a series of vicissitudes: the man who milked the cow often hadn't washed his hands: it was placed in a pail that was not adequately washed, the cow was often suffering from mastitis of the udder, which wasn't adequately washed either; the milk was often left for hours on end at room temperature, exposed to the elements before being distributed to the population via different channels. I can assure you that very often that milk had lost much of its nutritional value. This is a great truth . . .

" . . . Take the baking industry, for example. Logically enough, we have to devote all our efforts now to the mechanization of sugar-cane harvesting and to doing away with hoeing and other rudimentary agricultural methods. But when we get to the bottom of things we discover that bread-producing methods in this country are also prehistoric. Very soon no one is going to want to work as a baker in this country. With those old machines where the flour is kneaded, and with those ovens where the baker is baked together with the bread. Those crackers and that bread that you eat every day — for which you often have to stand in lines, also — are produced under the most incredible conditions of technological backwardness, by a large labour force which is hard to find. Because 1,800 students entered the University of Havana's School of Medicine this year, but not three students entered bakers' school. Not three! Who wants to study to be a baker? That's like asking who wants to study to be a cane-cutter . . .

"Therefore, we have to set up a practically all-new food industry, because I believe the people are right in desiring that a large part of our efforts be directed now toward meeting those needs — for food, footwear, clothing, etc.

"We have some new equipment. You have seen the plastic shoes that have been distributed, the first shoes made by the new machines. Let me give you an example. Some 19,000 shoemakers are turning out between eighteen and twenty million pairs of ordinary-type shoes every year — leather shoes, tennis shoes, and others. This new type of plastic shoe is going to solve many of our problems . . . The first new machines are now devoted to turning out plastic shower shoes for the cane-cutters so that they won't have to walk to the showers barefooted, and production will begin in January of shoes for school-children — that is, in the first quarter of the year. Beginning in the second quarter, production will be for the entire population. In that plant, one hundred and fifty women will make ten million pairs of shoes per year with just ten machines. Only one hundred and fifty women. The introduction of rubber in place of leather for soles, for example, liberates hundreds of thousands of hides which can be utilized in the production of more leather footwear. So, in 1970 we shall have that plant, staffed by one hundred and fifty women. In 1971 we can have another plant. By 1971 we can easily have a production of forty million pairs of shoes. Already in 1970 with those machines, and including the plastic shoes, we shall be producing nearly thirty million pairs. With how many more workers? By utilizing modern chemistry and modern techniques, three hundred women will produce twenty million pairs of shoes. But the same technology that produces the shoes will produce toys and containers of various sizes and for various uses.

"That is the course we have to follow. That is, the food industry and such light industries as textiles and footwear are the industries that must be given fundamental attention in the next five years. These needs must be met because the population in general is growing, the number of scholarship students is growing, the number of primary school students is growing, and the quantities needed are great.

"Of extraordinary importance are such branches of basic industry as power production. The need for electric power for the next few years will grow apace, with our need for dairy combines, rice mills, rice-drying plants, textile mills, automatic dairies — everything. And, when I spoke of the milk industry, I overlooked milking machines, of which we shall have to purchase several thousand in the next few years. Because that is another job, the job of milking cows at 4.00 in the morning, that nobody wants . . .

" . . . The needs of the construction industry are urgent and immediate. We must organize and equip hundreds of construction brigades in the coming years if we want to solve the infinite, immense and abysmal problems that we have on that front. And if anyone wants to know about this, he should go anywhere at all in the rôle of a person whom people think can solve their housing problems, and he will soon discover the real housing needs of this country. They are real and not imagined needs, but the possibility of solving them immediately is purely imaginary . . .

" . . . We expect to organize three hundred construction brigades between 1970 and 1972. And next year we will be purchasing the equipment for the first hundred.

"Everywhere we find a need for schools, as everyone knows from seeing children overcrowded and lacking adequate hygienic conditions. We need more day nurseries, more high-schools — because the number of high-school students coming up is enormous — more technological institutes of all sorts. The number of students who want to enter the institutes is also growing, and the country's need for them is also great.

"And all of the other things, such as movie houses and super-markets. For example, there are small towns in the interior where one suddenly sees something that resembles a procession. And one asks himself, 'But what's this? In what era are we living, and what are they celebrating?' But it is not a saint; it's the local movie house, where the people are forming a line four blocks long to see a film.

"It's true that, as revolutionaries, we've demonstrated our under-development by not getting films to all of our people. There's no doubt that we've demonstrated it, because I think ways and means exist to have movies reach all our people. But, being under-developed, we haven't managed it, in spite of having television, etc. And many of the films that are shown on television are so old as to be almost prehistoric, too.

"I confess that the revolution has proved itself incapable of solving some of these problems. Because, seeing those lines, one asks himself: 'Is it possible?' Just to see a movie, but they don't have a movie house or even a mini-movie house. All of a sudden every-one wants to go to the movies; no one has an inferiority complex anymore. Everyone has learned how to read the subtitles. People who never thought of going to a movie now want to go, but the movie house is nowhere to be seen. These are also realities, and the movie houses must be built. And this must be done with the prefabricated method . . .

" . . . We must also develop mining, especially nickel, as a source of foreign exchange.

"Our steel industry must undergo immediate development in order to produce the steel this country needs. Because you cannot imagine how much trouble this country goes through to buy steel. And we need steel for water tanks, equipment machinery, for every-thing. And our country is seriously considering the possibility of developing a steel industry based on natural resources such as chromium and, above all, nickel.

"We can produce the steel we need and develop the production of special steels as a very important export line with great possi-bilities. Because our country is abundantly supplied with nickel, which sells at very high prices and has a demand which — accord-ing to all signs — will maintain a satisfactory level in the near future. So we can think of the development of steel as a basic industry.

"And along with it goes the petrochemical industry, without which there cannot be a solution for many kinds of problems we must solve. And as a part of the petrochemical industry, the pro-duction of nitrogen and fertilizers for agriculture.

"And we are also thinking of developing in the near future the automotive industry to produce trucks; buses; and vehicles for basic economic and social needs, including motors, waterworks equipment, combines and tractors.

"We are not thinking of producing tractors to compete with General Motors, gentlemen. In the past, when there was talk of manufacturing some of those things, the 'wise men', the economic 'philosophers', used to say: 'How? We cannot produce under competitive conditions.' Well, gentlemen, we are going to compete against the conditions under which we have to acquire tractors today! Suffice it to say that, even importing the raw material and manufacturing the tractors ourselves, we could produce the equipment at twenty-five per cent the cost of the equipment we are importing now. At twenty-five per cent of what we are paying now for imported equipment! And not only the cost of importation. There is also the problem of spare parts. And we have had problems with spare parts from both capitalist and socialist countries, very serious problems. It's a tragedy, this problem of spare parts — from their purchase to shipment at the proper time — which, added to the very low technical level of our operators and mechanics and our reputation as destroyers of equipment — thanks to our abrupt jump from the ox to the tractor — constitutes a real tragedy. Sometimes we have dozens of pieces of equipment idle because we haven't been able to find spare parts for them, either socialist or capitalist-built. Until the spare parts arrive, the equipment is idle. Bulldozers and other heavy equipment standing idle because they lack treads, and things of that sort.

"For instance, in waterworks equipment, we have from seventy to eighty different kinds of motors. You can imagine what it means to service and maintain all of them.

"Our country is seriously thinking of developing an automotive industry, not to compete with anybody, but to insure a supply of the types of equipment we need, with the technical characteristics we want, the amount of spare parts we need, and to standardize the machinery.

"Because a country that in, let's say, 1980 is going to need 100,000 tractors can very well afford to have a factory to produce from 10,000 to 15,000 tractors a year, plus all the accessories they need.

"And the same thing is true in transport, with regard to buses and everything else. And that is the reason why our country is planning to develop that field. Even now, the comrades working in that field, with very scarce resources, with some lathes, have built loader-scrapers, pneumatic tampers and well-drilling equipment, and have been solving serious machinery problems.

"In Oriente Province's rice plan twenty scraper-loaders made in the Guanabo shop did a canal-digging job that would have required forty CD-8 bulldozers. They have also made pneumatic tampers needed in dam and road buildings, because rollers are very inefficient for road building. Machines weighing up to thirty-five, forty or fifty tons are needed to do a good job on highways and roads.

"We have been solving important problems in artisan-type shops. For example, three hundred deep-well pumps, of the kind that formerly had to be imported, were cast in the Lujan shop and assembled in Guanabo. And they are going to produce pneumatic tampers, well-drilling equipment, loader-scrapers and many other things. We simply have to shake off that idea that everything always has to be imported.

"We placed orders in Europe for one hundred machines for drilling wells, and eighteen months went by while they arrived one at a time by ship, and each one took up an enormous space on our docks. Yet, now, in February, we shall have one hundred of the same pieces of equipment built in Cuba. One hundred of them built in Cuba!

"Therefore, the automotive and agricultural machinery industry in general is one of the branches the country must develop, and work is being done in this direction.

"First, we must train the skilled personnel. An Electronics Institute, with a capacity for 2,500 students, with the equipment furnished by Sweden through UNESCO, will be established. The refrigeration industry will also be developed, and a technological institute will be created.

"Our country must also build shipyards in the coming years, in the next decade, inexorably, since here our situation is the same as with agricultural equipment.

"This country would need some two hundred and fifty ships of 10,000 ton displacement just to carry, say, in 1980, half of what would be coming in and out of it. And we either have our ships or we pay freight and continue to put up with all the inconveniences that the country has had in exporting and importing by chartering ships in the face of daily pressure and economic blockade from Yankee imperialists . . .

" . . . Cuba must develop not only its merchant fleet, but also its fishing fleet, a fleet that keeps growing rapidly and has enormous possibilities. This is another victory for the revolution in a country where the only fishing done was from rowboats either in Havana Bay or from the rocks near the sea-wall drive. That is the way it was done. That, and some vessels that resembled Christopher Columbus' caravels and were used to fish in the Gulf of Mexico. I am sure that you have seen them at one time or another on some romantic evening as they approached the port entrance. And today we have ships with a displacement of thousands of tons that bring frozen fish from thousands of miles away and carry crews over many thousands of miles . . .

" . . . In general and in essence, we have enumerated a series of basic and fundamental lines. But we could add dozens more. The paper industry and the printing industry must be developed. In short, there is a series of branches that must be included in the development possibilities for the next few years.

"A long-range plan is being studied. I don't think it will be perfect as it is just a beginning . . .

" . . . However, we can say that, in the main, the foundation for the country's food production, which was an objective of the battle of agriculture, has been laid. We will now launch into the development of industry in general in the coming years. And we will go into the development of our agriculture, a serious undertaking, we must say, in much better conditions than those we had this year or at the beginning of this decade.

"And, simultaneously, the problems of infrastructure. For example, the matter of ports, which is an imperative need. We are getting the equipment for the mechanization of our ports and working on plans to increase our ports' capacity, since it constitutes a serious bottleneck. Highway and road building is going strong. By 1970, this front will be fully equipped.

"Plans for high-speed train service between the western and eastern regions of the country are under study. A great many Soviet engineers who are going to help us draw up the project for the two-way express railroad have begun arriving.

"So we are preparing projects for roads, highways, railroads and ports and are already at work on the highway front. It will be completely equipped, as I was saying, by next year. The dams and irrigation sectors will be completely equipped by 1970, as well.

"We still have to provide the equipment for the port construction and mechanization brigades.

"We are very satisfied with the fact that such a large group of economists is being graduated . . .

" . . . Our economists of today are not men trying to help a firm make more money. It is a matter of making the most efficient use of the human, technical and material resources available to a country for the attaining of objectives that the country has set itself.

"An economist from the University accompanied a delegation that toured the main steel-producing countries of the world in search of technological data on steel production. Other teams of technicians, accompanied by economists, are doing the same for the sugar industry. And so there is plenty of work waiting for you everywhere, waiting for the graduates and for the undergraduates.

"You will always have to be studying. At the speed with which technology, science, control methods, leadership methods, analytical methods and other sciences are marching, anyone who stops studying for five years will find himself abysmally behind. You all know this. It isn't necessary to exhort anyone. The motivation offered by society itself, by life itself, by the tasks and struggle, are more than enough for everyone to understand the importance of study and self-improvement.

"A few hours ago we met here fortuitously with the students for this ceremony. What awaits them under the revolution is so new, so different, from the future faced by the student of the past, who, upon graduation, had to start thinking of what door he would knock on, to what shopkeeper he would appeal for a job that would allow him to vegetate.

"And vegetating isn't living. Living is having something to do, a goal, an objective, a task, a project to which to dedicate one's time, energy and life. And that is what you have; that is what the university students in our country have.

"And, if no one has any other questions, I hope you will permit me to bring this ceremony to a close.

Patria o muerte.
Venceremos."

Postscript

Cuba challenges the central doctrines of Western capitalism: that fear of poverty is a necessary incentive, that poor people are by and large lazy, that broad equality is a pipe dream, and — most important — that capitalism is the most efficient means of creating wealth with freedom.

Since this question of freedom plagues the whole third world, it needs definition from our point of view. One needs to distinguish between primary freedom — freedom to eat enough, to work, to become literate, to be healthy, to learn skills — and secondary freedom, such as two-party elections and an independent press. The West, having the first, is ready to go to war for the second. The third world suffers or benefits, or suffers that it may benefit, from this democratic concern ("We had to destroy the town to save it"), and left-wing revolutions launched in the name of bread are destroyed by right-wing *coups* in the name of freedom. In Latin America alone, between 1961–64, there were ten major right-wing *coups*, all supported by the United States.

There is a view that this right-wing reaction throughout the third world was provoked by Castro's extremism. Why couldn't he have sweetened the United States, dealt moderately with the US oil companies, and gone gently left? According to *Commerce*, a leading Indian business periodical: "While it is true that the Government of India would have been glad to see its proposal for refining Russian crude oil accepted by the [foreign] oil companies, it has not, unlike the Cuban Government, retaliated against them when they gave a firm negative reply. Dr Castro would have done a distinct service to all the capital-hungry and technologically backward under-developed countries had he retracted his step and followed India's example of respecting its agreements with the oil companies."

The gradualist road is tempting to everyone bored with revenge and hating bloody solutions, but what has gradualism achieved for the third world? Even conservative North American economists offer cold comfort: "The encouraging patterns of growth in the under-developed world admittedly hide much that remains to be done, even some things that seem never can be done. One of these is the gap in *per capita* income between rich and poor. Even if India were to grow at a *per capita* rate of four per cent, while the United States, for example, grew at two per cent *per capita*, the absolute levels would continue to widen. To illustrate, a four per cent growth rate would increase a *per capita* income of $100 to $104 in one year, or by $4, while a two per cent increase on a US *per capita* income of $4000 generates an increase of $80, twenty times the Indian increase ... Even at a four per cent *per capita* growth, highly optimistic for India, it would take nearly two hundred years to increase a $100 *per capita* income to $2,500, by which time Western relative standards will have shot still further ahead in absolute terms ... The widening gap problem has not been considered seriously in the US foreign aid programmes, because it is not only intractable to practical solution, but is also regarded as irrelevant to the development process as an average income earner who expects to achieve Rockefeller wealth status in his lifetime. Instead it is growth that is emphasised — i.e. a better living standard this year than last year ... A widening gap between rich nation and poor appears inevitable until we find catalysts hitherto unknown to man to produce innovative surges in growth in the less developed world." (Richard T. Ward, "Long Think on Development: a US view", *International Affairs*, January 1970.)

The chronic inferiority of the third world doesn't, of course, drop from heaven. If, for example, the US oil companies in India had agreed to refine Soviet crude, this would have been of considerable benefit to India. Why did they refuse? Because it would set off a chain reaction of similar demands throughout the third world and would cut their profits, which in turn would harm the prosperity of the United States and the West.

According to Michael Tanzer's authoritative book, *The Political Economy of International Oil* (page 46): "Without the overseas affiliates of the [US] oil companies, the US balance of payments deficit in 1964 would have been a quarter greater than it was . . . Great Britain's overseas oil investments have been the difference between a shaky solvency and bankruptcy."

The position is that the economic stability of the third world threatens the economic stability of the West. The ideal solution would be gradual levelling up, but this, as Ward pointed out, is no part of US foreign policy. The third world must be content with inferiority. Castro's Cuba is so important to countries like my own because it challenges this doctrine.